The Best of 50s TV

MALLARD
PRESS

An imprint of BDD Promotional Book Company, Inc.
666 Fifth Avenue, New York, New York 10103

The Best of 50s TV

Michael McCall

Previous pages: (l. to r.) The cast of Make Room For Daddy; Milton Berle; Jack Webb and Ben Alexander of Dragnet; and Perry Como. These pages: The stars of I Love Lucy: (left) William Frawley and Desi Arnaz; (right) Lucille Ball and Vivian Vance.

MALLARD PRESS

AN IMPRINT OF BDD PROMOTIONAL BOOK COMPANY, INC.
666 FIFTH AVENUE
NEW YORK, N.Y. 10103

MALLARD PRESS AND THE ACCOMPANYING DUCK LOGO ARE REGISTERED TRADEMARKS OF THE BDD PROMOTIONAL BOOK COMPANY, INC. REGISTERED IN THE U.S. PATENT OFFICE, COPYRIGHT © 1992.

FIRST PUBLISHED IN THE UNITED STATES OF AMERICA IN 1992 BY THE MALLARD PRESS.

ALL RIGHTS RESERVED.

Copyright © 1992 by M & M Books

ISBN 0-7924-5821-4

AN M&M BOOK
The Best of 50s TV was prepared and produced by M & M Books, 11 W. 19th Street, New York, New York 10011.

Project Director & Editor Gary Fishgall
Editorial Assistants Maxine Dormer, Ben D'Amprisi, Jr.
Copyediting and Proofreading Judith Rudnicki
Designer David Lunn
Separations and Printing Regent Publishing Services Ltd.

All of the photos in this volume are courtesy of Photofest, except for those on pages 54–55, which are courtesy of the Miss America Organization.

-CONTENTS-

4. Dramatic Series and Anthologies / 67

5. Variety Shows / 93

Acknowledgements / 112

Robert Young as Jim Anderson and Elinor Donahue as Betty Anderson in Father Knows Best.

Introduction

Television, it has been argued, is the most influential social invention since the printing press. It has changed not only the way people entertain themselves, but also how we interact and how we perceive ourselves, our neighbors, our nation, and our world. It affects all levels of our lives, from how we vote to how we dress.

Today, in our world of satellites, cables, remote controls, and VCRs, it may be hard to imagine a time without microwave images—but only if you're under 50. A half-century ago, the mention of television would have drawn the reaction, "What's that?" At the outset of World War II, only a few hundred television sets existed, mostly as the experimental toys of forward-thinking scientists and electronic engineers.

It was in 1947 that RCA began mass production of a seven-inch television screen for the common living room. At the time, the company's NBC network televised a live one-hour drama on Wednesday nights, two hours of sports on Monday and Friday, an hour of music and documentaries on Thursdays, and little else. The rival Dumont network provided a daily 30-minute children's program, a Monday night talent contest, a Tuesday night Western movie, and that's about it. CBS-TV consisted of one New York station with no regular programming. ABC was a radio network without television affiliates.

In the fall of 1947, NBC gambled by providing live coverage of baseball's World Series for the first time. The games were shown only in New York City, Schenectady, Philadelphia, and Washington, D.C. Some 3.9 million people watched, most of them in neighborhood bars, as the New York Yankees beat the Brooklyn Dodgers in a dramatic seven-game series. By the end of the year, 170,000 TV sets had been purchased.

In 1948, CBS and ABC joined NBC in offering nightly network programming. The shows were broadcast live along the East Coast and provided to affiliated stations by kinescope (a cheap, grainy version of film) in the Midwest and West. By the fall of that year, the revolution took hold, thanks largely to the comic antics of Milton Berle, host of *Texaco Star Theater*. The show's effect was comparable to today's Super Bowl Sunday—only it happened every Tuesday night. Streets emptied, and merchants experienced a dramatic decline in activity.

In 1949, NBC initiated live transmissions to the Midwest and, by the end of the year, one million television sets had been purchased. Two years later, both NBC and CBS relayed shows from New York to every corner of the country, and well over two million sets were in use. America was hooked.

In the beginning, a sense of experimentation dominated the airwaves. Sid Caesar and the cast of *Your Show of Shows* pushed the limits of improvisational comedy. George Burns reacted to his wife Gracie's antics by speaking directly to the camera, as if confiding in the viewer. Years later, *Saturday Night Live* and *It's Garry Shandling's Show* were described as revolutionary for employing these same techniques.

Other network fare evolved less creatively. Until the late 1940s, news programs consisted solely of newsreels with voice-over narration. By the 1950s, viewers could watch a solemn, middle-aged gentleman sitting behind a desk reading the news with little on-the-spot film footage. But with *See It Now*, Ed Murrow and Fred Friendly set the standard for in-depth news programs that latter-day programs like *60 Minutes* and *20/20* would follow. And by the decade's end Chet Huntley and David Brinkley were anchoring a mighty half-hour news roundup from Washington as well as New York and most stories were accompanied by film footage.

Color caught on slowly, too. A drawn-out battle over the specifications of color broadcasting ended in 1953, when the Federal Communications Commission accepted the standards set forth by RCA, which made the transmissions compatible to black-and-white sets. But color productions were expensive, and only RCA-owned NBC rushed into color series. With only a few such offerings, the public was slow to replace its recently purchased black-and-whites. It wasn't until 1962 that the number of color sets crossed the million mark in sales.

"And awa-a-a-ay we go!" Jackie Gleason of *The Jackie Gleason Show*.

At the start of the decade, television presented several high-quality anthology dramas featuring different scripts and casts each week. By the end of the decade, these shows had largely been replaced by situation comedies, Westerns, and serial dramas. The other early TV staple, the variety show with its assorted musical guests and ongoing comedy skits, endured longer but has largely vanished now as well.

Viewers established their preferences quickly, leaning decidedly toward certain formats designed by distinctive pioneers. There was the red-head named Lucy, whose scatterbrained schemes constantly confounded her husband and launched the situation comedy. There was the poker-faced Sergeant Joe Friday, a Los Angeles homicide detective whose just-the-facts manner initiated a trend toward realism in action dramas.

There was the quiz show that offered regular people the chance to win $64,000 by answering questions, then kept the cameras on them as tension mounted. There was the Old West marshal named Dillon, who maintained justice by imposing his gentle, indomitable presence on a rough-and-tumble town, thereby transforming the Western TV hero into a well-rounded, adult figure and inspiring dozens of less successful series exploiting the cowboy myth.

The medium's enormous impact on America was not predicted but was quickly felt. In 1952, a vice-presidential candidate turned to TV to try to salvage his career. Richard M. Nixon pleaded his case with a masterful, emotional speech which included a reference to the family cocker spaniel, Checkers. He not only avoided a scandal concerning the personal use of campaign donations, he became a national hero overnight and boosted the candidacy of his running mate, Dwight D. Eisenhower, who went on to win the election by an overwhelming majority.

The power of the cathode ray tube was obvious, and the molds had been cast. Pick almost any series from the 1960s to the 1990s, and its role model can be found in the era now known as the Golden Age of Television. A look back to the medium's first successful decade suggests that TV, as much as any other medium or product, reacts to public opinion and then imposes the tastes of the majority on a nation. It may be, as Bertrand Russell said, "Chewing gum for the eyes," but the flavor, or lack of it, has been dictated by those switching the channels.

Situation Comedies

I Love Lucy

Veteran film actress Lucille Ball spent three years in the late 1940s drawing laughs on a CBS radio show called *My Favorite Husband*. In it, the tall redhead played a ditzy housewife prone to bawling loudly when she didn't get her way.

In 1950, CBS told Ball that they'd like her to transfer her character to a TV series. But Ball wanted her husband, bandleader Desi Arnaz, to co-star. And she asked that production take place on the West Coast (nearly all TV series were created in New York at the time).

CBS frowned on both ideas. America wouldn't accept a Cuban as her husband, they said, and coast-to-coast live transmissions weren't possible from Los Angeles. So Ball and Arnaz borrowed $5,000 to set up a production company and developed their own pilot. They taped the program on film in Los Angeles before a live audience (all firsts for a TV series).

CBS accepted the show in 1951 with a few modifications. The couple's names were changed from Lucy and Larry Lopez to Lucy and Ricky Ricardo, and

(Previous page) *Phil Silvers as Sgt. Ernie Bilko in* The Phil Silvers Show.

One of the best remembered episodes of the series found Ethel and Lucy wrapping candy on an assembly line. In order to keep up, they ate the product. Then their supervisor, seen here, told the offstage workers to "Speed it up!"

they would live in a small, middle-class Manhattan apartment. Vivian Vance and William Frawley were added as Ethel and Fred Mertz, the Ricardo's neighbors, landlords, and best friends.

The premise wasn't very different from other TV comedies. Lucy Ricardo was a scatterbrained wife whose adventures continually exasperated her husband. What distinguished *I Love Lucy* were the superb plots, the inventive gags, and the irresistible mannerisms of the stars, especially Ball's physical clowning.

The show was an immediate hit, ranking number one for four of its six seasons, coming in third the first year and second in its fifth year. *I Love Lucy* was the first program to be seen in 10 million homes, and when the couple ended the show in 1957, it was still rated the most popular program in the nation. In the 1960s, Ball returned to TV with two other highly successful series: *The Lucy Show* (1962–1969), and *Here's Lucy* (1969–1974).

I Love Lucy (CBS), 1951–1957. Lucy Ricardo: Lucille Ball, Ricky Ricardo: Desi Arnaz, Ethel Mertz: Vivian Vance, Fred Mertz: William Frawley, Little Ricky Ricardo: Richard Keith (Keith Thibodeaux) (1956–1957).

The central setting for I Love Lucy was the Ricardo's Manhattan apartment, clearly recognizable in this photo, along with the regular cast—(l. to r.) William Frawley as Fred Mertz, Lucille Ball as Lucy Ricardo, Vivian Vance as Ethel Mertz, and Desi Arnaz as Ricky Ricardo.

The Donna Reed Show

In 1958, Oscar-winning actress Donna Reed came to television as Donna Stone, a loving housewife and mother of two. Her pediatrician husband, Alex, was played by Carl Betz.

Donna Reed was a well-known film actress in the 1950s: she had starred alongside Jimmy Stewart in the popular Christmas movie *It's a Wonderful Life,* and she won an Academy Award for her role in *From Here to Eternity.* To many Americans, however, she is best remembered for small-screen work as Donna Stone, the loving, all-American mother who was as wholesome as fresh cream.

Donna Stone lived in the small, peaceful town of Hilldale with her pediatrician husband Alex (Carl Betz) and her two rambunctious children, the teen-aged Mary (Shelly Fabares) and younger brother Jeff (Paul Petersen). The shows, more wholesome than funny, evolved around small family problems, busybody neighbors, and the children as they made there way through school, dating, minor illnesses, and little white lies. Because Alex was usually running off to attend to patients, Donna was left to deal with the various crises on her own.

The ABC show barely survived its first season. Instead of canceling it, however, the network shifted it from Wednesday to Thursday night, where it fared better. In 1962, Mary went off to college, and Shelly Fabares scored a top pop hit, "Johnny Angel." She left the series at the end of that season.

Paul Petersen attempted to match Fabares' recording success, premiering his single, "She Can't Find the Keys," as part of a dream sequence in a 1962 program in which he imagined himself as a teen recording idol. It, too, became a hit, and Petersen followed it in 1963 with "My Dad," a song about Alex Stone.

After Fabares left, the Stones adopted an eight-year-old orphan, Trisha, played by Patty Petersen, Paul's sister. She stayed until the series ended in 1966.

The Donna Reed Show (ABC), 1958–1966. Donna Stone: Donna Reed, Alex Stone: Carl Betz, Mary Stone: Shelley Fabares (1958–1963), Jeff Stone: Paul Petersen, Trisha Stone: Patty Petersen (1963–1966), Dr. Dave Kelsey: Bob Crane (1963–1966), Midge Kelsey: Ann McCrea (1963–1966).

Until Shelley Fabares left the series in 1963, many of the show's episodes focused on the turbulent teen-age years of her character, Mary Stone. She is seen here (right) with Reed and Jimmy Hawkins, who played Scottie, Mary's steady boyfriend.

The Phil Silvers Show

In 1951, veteran comic actor Phil Silvers starred in a Broadway farce, *Top Banana*, about a vaudeville comedian who made it big in television. Four years later, Silvers himself did just that in *The Phil Silvers Show*, appearing as the brash, fast-talking Sergeant Bilko, a military man constantly on the make.

Bilko was an urban hustler stuck at fictional Fort Baxter, Kansas, and he filled his hours creating schemes, most of which were designed to earn him fast money or help him avoid hard work. He repeatedly outsmarted his hot-tempered, self-important superior, Col. John Hall (Paul Ford), while, at the same time, manipulating the members of his platoon into furthering his schemes. In the end, though, Bilko's plots never truly cheated anyone, and he was ultimately harmless and often softhearted.

Col. John Hall (Paul Ford) was simply no match for the fast-talking Bilko.

More often than not, the patsy in Bilko's schemes was the sweet, naive Pvt. Duane Doberman, played by Maurice Gosfield.

Sgt. Ernie Bilko (Phil Silvers, center) may have been in charge of the motor pool at fictional Fort Baxter, but his real mission in life was cooking up get-rich schemes for himself and his cronies, Cpl. Henshaw (Allan Melvin, seated left) and Cpl. Barbella (Harvey Lembeck, seated right).

When introduced in 1955, the series was called *You'll Never Get Rich*, but CBS changed the title two months later to reflect its star's popularity. The cast was as colorful as its lead character: Harvey Lembeck and Allan Melvin played Silver's co-conspirators Cpl. Rocco Barbella and Cpl. Henshaw; Maurice Gosfield portrayed the bumbling, overweight Pvt. Duane Doberman; Joe E. Ross was the excitable Sgt. Rupert Ridzick; and Elisabeth Fraser appeared as Bilko's occasional girlfriend, Sgt. Joan Hogan.

The show never cracked the top twenty programs during its four-year run. It proved more enduring in syndication, usually appearing under the title *Sergeant Bilko*.

The Phil Silvers Show (CBS), 1955–1959. Sgt. Ernie Bilko: Phil Silvers, Col. John Hall: Paul Ford, Cpl. Rocco Barbella: Harvey Lembeck, Cpl. Henshaw: Allan Melvin, Pvt. Duane Doberman: Maurice Gosfield, Sgt. Rupert Rudzik: Joe E. Ross, Sgt. Joan Hogan: Elisabeth Fraser (1955–1958), Pvt. Sam Fender: Herbie Faye, Pvt. Dino Paparelli: Billy Sands, Nell Hall: Hope Sansberry.

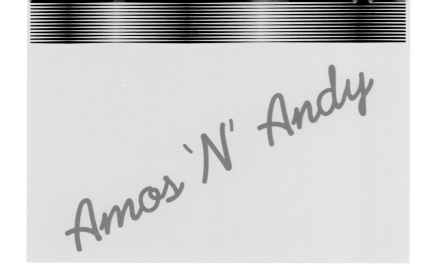

Amos 'N' Andy

Amos 'N' Andy ranked as America's most popular, longest-running comedy series on radio for the two decades prior to the advent of network television. Amos Jones and Andy Hogg Brown were created and played on radio by Freeman Goodsen and Charles Correll, two white vaudeville comedians who based their characters on old-fashioned, black-face skits.

Launched in 1929, Amos 'N' Andy proved to be an immediate hit, drawing an estimated 40 million listeners at its peak—even President Calvin Coolidge told aides he was not to be disturbed when the show was on the air. The popularity of Amos 'N' Andy helped establish NBC radio as America's preeminent broadcaster in the 1930s and 1940s.

In 1951, the CBS television network attempted to advance on NBC by bidding for its rival's biggest stars. CBS offered an astounding $1 million to Goodsen and Correll for the TV rights to Amos 'N' Andy, thereby stealing the show. To bring the series to the tube, CBS began a highly publicized search for black actors to take over the roles. Alvin Childress was hired to play Amos, a hard-working, level-headed Harlem taxi driver who co-owned a one-cab firm with his friend Andy, a well-meaning but lazy oaf constantly being conned by others. George "Kingfish" Stevens (Tim Moore) was usually the one swindling Andy, using his role as head of the fraternal Mystic Knights of the Sea to convince Andy that he was working in both of their best interests.

Although it ranked number 13 among all programs its first year, Amos 'N' Andy lasted only two seasons. However, the shows remained popular in reruns through the 1950s. In 1966, CBS withdrew Amos 'N' Andy from syndication because of pressure from civil rights groups, which protested that the characters perpetuated racial stereotypes.

Amos 'N' Andy focused on the mishaps of a hard-working taxi driver named Amos Jones (Alvin Childress, left), his well-meaning but not too bright friend, Andy Brown (Spencer Williams, Jr., right), and the head of their fraternal lodge, George "Kingfish" Stevens (Tim Moore).

Amos 'N' Andy (CBS), 1951–1953, Amos Jones: Alvin Childress, Andrew "Andy" Hogg Brown: Spencer Williams, Jr., George "The Kingfish" Stevens: Tim Moore, Sapphire Stevens: Ernestine Wade, Lightnin': Horace Stewart, Sapphire's Mama: Amanda Randolph, Madame Queen: Lillian Randolph.

For the moment at least it seems that elder son Wally (Tony Dow) has the rest of the Cleaver clan "peeved" at him. They are (l. to r.) Jerry Mathers as the Beaver, Hugh Beaumont as Ward Cleaver, and Barbara Billingsley as June Cleaver.

Leave It to Beaver gave viewers the novel opportunity of looking at a comfortable middle-class family from the point of view of its youngest son, Theodore, known to all as "Beaver."

Jerry Mathers, who played the Beaver, brought a charming naturalness to the role of a well-meaning, curious youngster whose antics repeatedly landed him in trouble with his parents, Ward and June (Hugh Beaumont and Barbara Billingsley). Beaver also looked upon the actions of his hip older brother Wally (Tony Dow) with skeptical awe. He didn't understand Wally's interest in girls or why he fussed so much with hygiene and clothes, but he was amazed at how Wally managed so well with schoolwork and his parents.

The family lived in the fictional town of Mayfield, and of the many friends to join the two boys over the years, the most memorable were Beaver's chubby pal, Larry Mondello (Rusty Stevens), and Wally's hooligan buddy, Eddie Haskell (Ken Osmond), the latter tending to bully Beaver and his pals while treating Mr. and Mrs. Cleaver with overbearing, phony politeness.

The show ran one season on CBS starting in 1957, then was picked up by ABC, where it remained until 1963. By that time, Beaver was in high school and Wally was attending college, and the cuteness had lost its appeal. The program never made the top twenty and has proven much more popular in syndication than it was during its original run.

Leave It to Beaver CBS, 1957–1958; ABC, 1958–1963. Theodore "Beaver" Cleaver: Jerry Mathers, Wally Cleaver: Tony Dow, June Cleaver: Barbara Billingsley, Ward Cleaver: Hugh Beaumont, Eddie Haskell: Ken Osmond, Clarence "Lumpy" Rutherford: Frank Bank (1958–1963), Larry Mondello: Rusty Stevens (1958–1960), Whitey Whitney: Stanley Fafara, Miss Landers: Diane Brewster (1958–1962), Fred Rutherford: Richard Deacon.

Leave It to Beaver

The George Burns and Gracie Allen Show

The
George
Burns
and Gracie Allen
Show

From 1950 until October 1952, *The George Burns and Gracie Allen Show* appeared on alternate Thursday nights, becoming a weekly program in its third season. It ranked among TV's Top 20 for the only time in its fourth year, the 1954/55 season. The

A successful vaudeville and radio team, real-life husband and wife George Burns and Gracie Allen brought their delightful brand of humor to the small screen in 1950. The show ended eight years later, when Gracie decided to retire.

George Burns and his wife Gracie Allen first became popular as vaudeville performers in the 1920s. Then, in the early 1930s, as vaudeville theaters began closing, they slipped out the door in time to enter the new entertainment phenomenon, radio. For the next two decades, *The George Burns and Gracie Allen Show* ranked among America's most popular radio programs and helped CBS get a foothold as a national broadcasting network.

In 1950, CBS coaxed husband and wife to transfer their show to television, where their programs closely followed the format of the radio series: Burns usually opened with a short monologue which would conclude with the setup for his wife's current escapade, which often involved her neighbor, Blanche Morton (Bea Benaderet). The situation comedy would then unfold, with Allen acting delightfully scatterbrained and Burns watching with loving, unflappable tolerance. Burns also narrated the action, turning to the camera, cigar in hand, to add his wry comments. (The technique was revived in the late 1980s on *It's Garry Shandling's Show*.

The series may best be remembered for its traditional ending segment, featuring Burns and Allen in a back-and-forth vaudeville routine featuring George playing the straight man to Gracie's perfectly mixed-up wordplay. It then closed with the classic "Say Goodnight, Gracie."

series ended in 1958, not because CBS canceled it, but because Allen decided to retire. Burns hosted his own show for one more season on CBS.

The George Burns and Gracie Allen Show (CBS), 1950–1958. George Burns: himself, Gracie Allen: herself, Blanche Morton: Bea Benaderet, Harry Morton: Hal March (1950/51), John Brown (1951), Fred Clark (1951–1953), Larry Keating (1953–1958), Harry Von Zell: himself, Ronnie Burns: himself, Judi Meredith: herself.

Highlighting the Burns-and-Allen routines were Gracie's rambling stories about members of her family, which always left George confused.

Make Room For Daddy centered around the home life of nightclub entertainer Danny Williams (Danny Thomas). His wife for the first three years of the series was played by Jean Hagen.

Make Room For Daddy

When Danny Thomas made his living as a nightclub entertainer, his family became accustomed to his spending extended periods on the road. Whenever he was due home, the children prepared for his arrival by changing bedrooms. In time, the routine developed into a family joke: "Make room for Daddy."

In 1953, Thomas began starring in a situation comedy about a nightclub comedian and singer named Danny Williams who also was a husband and father. The episodes humorously examined his attempts to be a paternal figure and to maintain his position as head of the household despite his prolonged absences. Remembering the family joke, Thomas suggested the show's name: *Make Room For Daddy*.

As a father, Danny Williams was ostentatious yet tender. At home, his two children were the stars, continually letting the air out of his ego and reminding him of life's more basic truths and simpler joys. When the show began, Rusty Hamer was a bratty six-year-old, Rusty, and Sherry Jackson was a lovably precocious 11-year-old, Terry. (The show ran long enough for her character to get married on the air.) Jean Hagen played Thomas' wife, Margaret Williams, until 1956. When the actress left the series, her character died, and Williams remained a widower until 1958. Then he remarried, with actress Marjorie Lord playing his second wife, Kathy. Actress Angela Cartwright made her TV debut as Linda Williams, Kathy's daughter by a previous marriage. Other memorable characters introduced on the show included elevator operator Jose Jimenez (Bill Dana) and Danny's Uncle Tonoose (Hans Conreid).

In 1957, the show moved from ABC to CBS, and the name officially became *The Danny Thomas Show*. As such, it enjoyed its best ratings ever, coming in at number two for the year and remaining in the top ten until 1964, when Thomas decided to call it quits so that he could devote more of his attention to his highly successful production company.

Make Room For Daddy (The Danny Thomas Show) (ABC), 1953–1957; (CBS), 1957–1964. Danny Williams: Danny Thomas, Rusty Williams: Rusty Hamer, Terry Williams: Sherry Jackson (1953–1958), Penney Parker (1959–1960), Margaret Williams: Jean Hagen (1953–1956), Kathy "Clancey" Williams: Marjorie Lord (1957–1964), Linda Williams: Angela Cartwright (1957–1964).

In 1958 Danny Williams remarried. His second wife was played by Marjorie Lord, and her daughter by a previous marriage introduced Angela Cartwright. They are seen here with Rusty Hamer, who played Williams' son, and a furry friend.

For more than a decade, Eve Arden had honed her sharp comic edge as a sarcastic, wise-cracking woman, working in vaudeville, in films, and on radio. Then in 1948, she took on her most famous role as Connie Brooks in the situation comedy, *Our Miss Brooks.*

Originating on CBS radio, *Our Miss Brooks* was brought to television 1952 and continued to air on both media through 1956. Connie Brooks was an indomitable English teacher at Madison High, respected by her students, including the doting, naive Walter Denton (Richard Crenna), and despised by the grouchy, pompous principal, Osgood P. Conklin (Gale Gordon). Miss Brooks also furtively pursued the handsome, painfully shy biology teacher, Philip Boynton (Robert Rockwell).

After three successful seasons, Madison High was torn down to make room for a new highway, and Miss Brooks transferred to Mrs. Nestor's Private Elementary School. Alas, so did her nemesis, principal Conklin. For half of the 1955 season, actor Gene Barry played gym coach Gene Talbot, who turned the tables on Miss Brooks, chasing her for a change. But the ratings fell, and Barry left as Rockwell returned to revive his role as Philip Boynton. Nevertheless, the magic seemed to have been left behind at Madison High, and the program was canceled in 1956.

Eve Arden played the indomitable English teacher Connie Brooks on radio and television. She is seen here doing her bit for Madison High when the janitor fails to come to work.

Our Miss Brooks (CBS), 1952–1956. Connie Brooks: Eve Arden, Osgood Conklin: Gale Gordon, Philip Boynton: Robert Rockwell, Walter Denton: Richard Crenna (1952–1955), Harriet Conklin: Gloria McMillan (1952–1955), Margaret Davis: Jane Morgan, Gene Talbot: Gene Barry (1955/56), Mrs. Nestor: Nana Bryant (1955), Isabel Randolph (1956).

Brooks was a continual irritant to principal Osgood P. Conkling (Gale Gordon, second from the right). In her present predicament, she doesn't seem to be receiving any help from her doting student, Walter Denton (Richard Crenna, left), or the biology teacher, Philip Boynton (Robert Rockwell).

This genial series focused on the "adventures" of the foursome pictured here—(clockwise from left) Harriet Nelson, David Nelson, Ricky Nelson, and Ozzie Nelson. Although Ozzie had been a bandleader in real life, he seemed to have no job whatsoever in the show.

The Adventures of Ozzie and Harriet

Ozzie Nelson had been a star quarterback at Rutgers University in the 1920s and a popular bandleader in the 1930s. His wife, the former Harriet Hilliard, had been a singer in his band. In the 1940s, the two turned to radio, and Nelson became the creator, director, writer, and star of a hit series.

In *The Adventures of Ozzie and Harriet*, however, Nelson did little more than work in his backyard and tend to his family. The program never indicated that Ozzie or Harriet held a job. Instead, the attention focused on the development of their two sons.

In 1949, Nelson's real-life children, David and Ricky, replaced the two child actors on the series. It was an important move, especially when ABC turned the program into a TV show in 1952.

For the next 14 years, David and Ricky grew up on camera. Ricky, the more famous of the two, began as an 11-year-old with a crew cut, turned into a rock 'n' roll star and teen idol, then left the show as a 25-year-old husband and father. The show followed David through law school and Ricky through pop stardom—he performed a song in nearly every episode after 1957. When the sons married, their wives joined the cast. David's wife, June Blair, first appeared in 1961, and Ricky's wife, Kris Harmon, followed in 1964.

The focus on the second generation continued until the end. The touching final episode in 1966 featured Ozzie suggesting to Harriet that they transform the boys' old bedroom into a game room, complete with pool table. Harriet opposed, and her sentiment won out.

The Adventures of Ozzie and Harriet (ABC), 1952–1966. Ozzie Nelson: himself, Harriet Nelson: herself, David Nelson: himself, Ricky Nelson: himself, June Nelson: herself (1961–1966), Kris Nelson: herself (1964–1966), "Thorny" Thornberry: Don DeFore (1952–1961), Joe Randolph: Lyle Talbot (1956–1966), Clara Randolph: Mary Jane Croft (1956–1966), Darby: Parley Baer (1955–1961), Doc Williams: Frank Cady (1954–1965).

As David (left) and Ricky matured, the show increasingly focused on them and their friends, thus bringing in a younger viewing audience. Ricky's singing career didn't hurt either. The young lady they are fighting over here is Luana Patten.

The wholesome family series, Father Knows Best starred Robert Young as a small-town insurance agent, Jim Anderson. His family consisted of (l. to r.) elder daughter Betty (Elinor Donahue), younger daughter Kathy (Lauren Chapin), wife Margaret (Jane Wyatt), and son Bud (Billy Grey).

Father Knows Best

In 1949, when Robert Young originally took the role of Jim Anderson on the radio serial *Father Knows Best*, the character was like many other fictional fathers of the time, a bumbling but well-meaning figure easily manipulated by his children and spouse.

However, Jim Anderson gradually grew more responsible and thoughtful, and the Anderson family came to represent the wholesome ideal of the well-adjusted middle American family, setting the tone for several successful family sitcoms to follow.

In 1954, CBS brought the popular radio series to television, with Young the only actor surviving the transition. But the network canceled the show after one season, a decision that drew a storm of protest letters, many of which suggested the show be aired earlier than 10 p.m. Sunday so that children could enjoy it. NBC adroitly picked up the program and moved it to 8:30 Wednesday night, where it thrived for five years.

Jim Anderson worked as an insurance agent in the peaceful small town of Springfield, where he lived with his wife Margaret (Jane Wyatt) and three children—Betty (Elinor Donahue), James, Jr. (Billy Gray), and Kathy (Lauren Chapin). The kids all had cute nicknames—Princess, Bud, and Kitten, respectively—and most shows featured Jim coming home from work, removing his jacket, slipping on a sweater, and solving some minor family problem with warm understanding and gentle advice.

In 1958, after reaching the top 20 rankings for the first time the previous season, *Father Knows Best* returned to CBS. It continued to grow in popularity, climbing to number six among network shows in the 1959/60 season. That year, Young announced he was leaving the series, having grown tired of the role. CBS continued to run reruns in prime time for two more seasons, and ABC picked up syndicated reruns for prime-time telecast for one last season in 1962. Young returned to TV in 1969 to star for seven years as kindly old Marcus Welby, M.D.

Father Knows Best (CBS), 1954/55, 1958–1962; (NBC) 1955–1958. Jim Anderson: Robert Young, Margaret Anderson: Jane Wyatt, Betty "Princess" Anderson: Elinor Donahue, James "Bud" Anderson: Billy Gray, Kathy "Kitten" Anderson: Lauren Chapin, Miss Thomas: Sarah Selby.

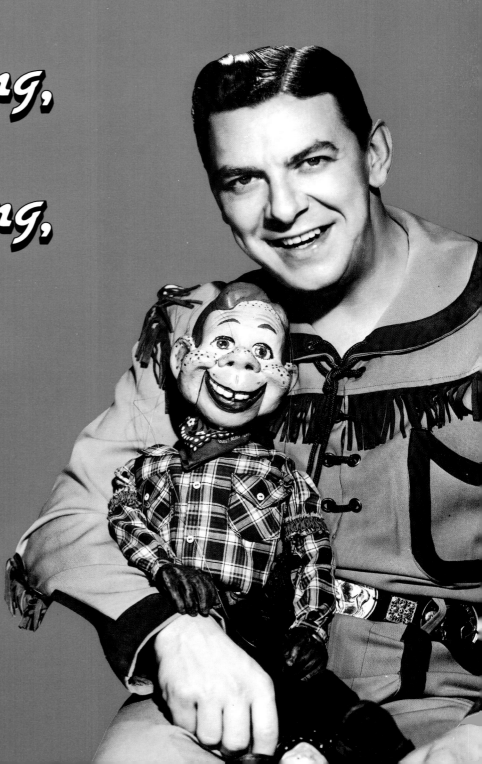

2

Children's Programming, Daytime Programming, and Game Shows

Chicago radio personality Fran Allison found national stardom when she joined forces with two puppets—Kukla, a bulbous-nosed worrywart, and Ollie, an eternally optimistic dragon with one tooth. They are seen here with the creator and voice of the puppets, Burr Tillstrom.

(Previous page) Buffalo Bob Smith and Howdy Doody.

Kukla, Fran & Ollie

Puppeteer Burr Tillstrom named his homemade entertainment troupe the "Kuklapolitan Players" in 1936, after Russian ballerina Tamara Toumanova saw his puppets and exclaimed "Kukla," the Russian word for doll.

Tillstrom's puppets performed on TV as early as 1939 on an experimental station in Chicago. In 1947, his most popular creations— Kukla and Oliver J. Dragon—were given their own Chicago TV series, *Junior Jamboree*. They were joined by Chicago radio personality Fran Allison, a former nightclub singer who communicated with good-natured enthusiasm with her wooden friends.

NBC began telecasting the show across the Midwest late in 1948, and the newly crowned *Kukla, Fran & Ollie* series grew along with the network's technology. By 1949, the show could be seen on the East Coast, and by 1951 the network was airing the show coast-to-coast for 15 minutes each weeknight.

The show was always performed live and usually without a script— exceptions came during more elaborate productions, such as the trio's version of *The Mikado*. Kukla was a solemn worrywart with a bulbous nose. Oliver J. "Ollie" Dragon was a lighthearted, eternally optimistic dragon with one tooth. Fran, the show's only human, was an engaging, youthful woman who stood in front of a small, elevated stage and conversed with the puppets. Tillstrom provided the puppet's voices. From time to time he also created other characters for the show's skits, ranging from ex–opera star Madame Ophelia Oglepuss to the droopy-eared mailman, Fletcher Rabbit.

In 1952, NBC moved the show from its daily prime-time spot to a weekly series on Sunday afternoons. In 1954, it was acquired by ABC which switched it back to a 15-minute nightly presentation on Mondays through Fridays. The program ended in 1957.

Kukla, Fran & Ollie (NBC), 1948–1954; (ABC), 1954–1957. Host: Fran Allison.

Producers Allen Ludden and Grant Tinker originated *College Bowl* as a radio series in 1953. Known then as *College Quiz Bowl*, the show featured two panels of four students each. The teams, each of which represented a U.S. university, competed against one another in a series of fast-paced rounds of questions and answers.

In 1959, when CBS brought the program to television on Saturday afternoons, it was billed as *The General Electric College Bowl* (after its sponsor), and Ludden assumed the role of host. In 1963, the series moved to NBC, Robert Earle took over from Ludden, and the name was shortened to *College Bowl*.

The game itself was simple. The student panels tried to answer a series of "toss-up" and multiple-part questions, amassing points for each correct response along the way. The winning team received $1,500 in scholarship funds and returned the following week to face another collegiate opponent, while the losing players took home $500 in scholarship money.

The series was canceled in 1970, but in 1984, NBC featured a prime-time tribute, the *30th Anniversary College Bowl National Championship*, hosted by Pat Sajak of *Wheel of Fortune*. The Disney Channel presented an updated *College Bowl '87* with Dick Cavett as host. It started in September 1987 and was canceled in December of that year.

College Bowl (CBS), 1959–1963; (NBC), 1963–1970. Host: Allen Ludden (1959–1962), Robert Earle (1962–1970).

From 1959 to 1962, Allen Ludden hosted the game that each week pitted players from two universities against one another in a series of fast-paced rounds of questions and answers.

Lassie

Lassie began her 17-year TV career as a companion to a young farm boy, Jeff Miller (Tommy Rettig), who lived with his widowed mother, Ellen Miller (Jan Clayton), and grandfather (George Cleveland).

Lassie Come Home, Eric Knight's best-selling 1940 novel, launched the story of a remarkably loyal and intelligent collie whose heroic exploits would turn her into a multimedia star and one of history's most famous fictional dogs.

Lassie starred in several movies and on radio before CBS made her a television star. In truth, there were six Lassies over the years, as well as a few stunt dogs, all males and all trained by Rudd Weatherwax. The collie's masters changed almost as often as the dogs, as Lassie moved through several families and locations over her prime-time run of 17 seasons.

On TV, Lassie began as a companion to a young farm boy, Jeff Miller (Tommy Rettig), who lived near the town of Calverton with his widowed mother, Ellen Miller (Jan Clayton), and grandfather (George Cleveland). In 1957, Lassie rescued a runaway orphan named Timmy (Jon Provost), who moved in with the Millers. That fall, Gramps died suddenly and the Millers sold the farm to the childless Martin family (June Lockhart and Hugh Reilly), who took in Timmy and Lassie.

In 1964, the Martins bought a farm in Australia and left Lassie with an elderly family friend. The caretaker soon died, and forest ranger Corey Stuart (Robert Bray) took over. He was the first in a succession of rangers who looked after the collie and led her to a life of even greater danger and excitement. The series was canceled in 1971, and spent three years in independent syndication.

Lassie (CBS), 1954–1971. Jeff Miller: Tommy Rettig (1954–1957), Ellen Miller: Jan Clayton (1954–1957), Gramps Miller: George Cleveland (1954–1957), Doc Weaver: Arthur Space (1954–1964), Timmy: Jon Provost (1957–1964), Ruth Martin: Cloris Leachman (1957–1958), Paul Martin: John Shepodd (1957–1958), Hugh Reilly (1958–1964), Cully Wilson: Andy Clyde (1958–1964), Corey Stuart: Robert Bray (1964–1969), Scott Turner: Jed Allan (1968–1970), Bob Erickson: Jack De Mave.

In 1957, Lassie rescued a runaway orphan named Timmy (Jon Provost). The following season dog and boy began to share their adventures with the childless couple (June Lockhart and Hugh Reilly) who took them in.

It must be Monday—"Fun with Music Day"
—as Jimmie Dodd leads a pack of the
Mousketeers in a rousing song.

The Mickey Mouse Club

The *Mickey Mouse Club* was film producer Walt Disney's second television creation, a weekday children's program introduced one year after the prime-time *Disneyland* series. The show, which was named for Disney's best-known cartoon character, starred a large, constantly changing cast of cheerful child performers known as the Mouseketeers. It was the only daily children's show not hosted by an adult (as in *Captain Kangaroo* or *Howdy Doody*'s Buffalo Bob). It also was the only children's show to feature serials, including two popular Hardy Boys' mysteries and three "Adventures of Spin and Marty," about two boys at a western summer camp known as the Triple R Ranch.

The Mouseketeers wore caps with mouse ears and T-shirts with their names emblazoned in big letters. They danced, sang, starred in skits and short serials, and introduced guest stars and cartoons. More than 40 children appeared as Mouseketeers over the show's four original seasons, with Annette Funicello being the best remembered. Filling out the cast were two adults, actor Jimmie Dodd and Disney writer-animator Roy Williams.

The series ran for an hour a day during its first two years, then for 30 minutes in its final two. The format depended on the day: Monday was "Fun with Music Day," Tuesday was "Guest Star Day," Wednesday was "Anything Can Happen Day," Thursday was "Circus Day" (featuring Disney cartoon character Jiminy Cricket), and Friday was "Talent Roundup Day."

The Mickey Mouse Club (ABC), 1955–1959.

Although The Mickey Mouse Club was an ensemble show, young Annette Funicello became the popular favorite among the Mousketeers. She went on to make several Disney films and the "beach" movies with Frankie Avalon.

Once a player reached the $8,000 level on *The $64,000 Question*, he or she moved into the isolation booth. That is where young Robert Strom is in this photo as he listens intently to a question posed by host Hal March. Strom, whose category was science, won $192,000 on the program on April 16, 1957.

The $64,000 Question

The *$64,000 Question* ushered in a brief, highly popular era of big-stakes quiz shows. Beginning in the summer of 1955, the CBS prime-time series took a successful radio program, *The $64 Question,* and inflated the potential winnings. It became an instant hit, becoming the only program to unseat *I Love Lucy* as top-rated series of the year, a feat the quiz show pulled off during its first full season (1955/1956).

The way the game worked was simple. Each contestant selected a topic on which he or she claimed to be an expert. The initial correct answer paid one dollar and the winnings doubled thereafter for each correct response. At any time, the contestant could pull out and take home whatever winnings had been earned at that point. Those who progressed to the $8,000 level moved into an isolation booth to allow for greater concentration. This kept contestants from hearing answers shouted by audience members, but it also heightened the drama of the quiz.

The first $64,000 winner was a Marine captain, Richard McCutchen, an expert in gastronomy. The second top winner was psychologist Dr. Joyce Brothers, a boxing authority, who went on to become a TV celebrity. Other winners included actress Barbara Feldon, a Shakespeare specialist, jockey Billy Pearson (art), 11-year-old Robert Strom (science), housewife Catherine Kreitzer (the Bible), New Yorker Redmond O'Hanlon (Shakespeare), and Bronx shoemaker Gino Prato (opera).

The successful series screeched to a halt in 1958 amid a scandal involving game shows which coached certain contestants to guarantee colorful winners. NBC's *Dotto* was the first show implicated when a contestant discovered that a rival's notes included answers to the questions. Then Howard Stempfel, a contestant on *Twenty-One*, revealed he'd been coached to win, as had Charles Van Doren, a Columbia University professor of literature whose high-profile winnings led to a on-air job with the *Today* show. When the scandal broke, Van Doren was fired from both the university and the TV program.

The *$64,000 Question* (CBS), 1955–1958. Host: Hal March, Assistant: Lynn Dollar (1955–1957), Pat Donovan (1958).

You Bet Your Life

You Bet Your Life paraded as a quiz show, and indeed guests did answer questions and could win money, but the primary purpose of the program was to showcase the quick, hilarious wit of host Groucho Marx, one of America's greatest humorists. Marx surprised many peers by accepting the job as host of the original radio version of *You Bet Your Life* in 1947. Three years later, NBC brought the program to prime-time television.

The shows opened with announcer George Fenneman introducing "the one, the only—Groucho Marx." The comic then traded a few pointed comments with his straight man before bringing on the first contestant. The subsequent short interview conducted by Marx was often the highlight of the show, with the famous wit shooting good-natured barbs at his willing guest (or guests, as couples or relatives could compete as teams).

Fenneman also introduced a "secret word" at the outset of each show. If the contestants used the word at any time, a stuffed duck would drop by wire from the ceiling with a one hundred dollar prize. The quiz consisted of questions from a category chosen by the guests, who bet all or part of a sum of money given them at the outset of the program. Those who lost it all were given consolation prizes.

The programs were filmed, which was unusual in those days, but the process allowed Marx the opportunity to let the interviews ramble on as he probed for good material, the best of which could be edited into a seamless whole later. Filming also gave editors a chance to excise the host's occasional off-color remarks before airtime. From 1950 until 1958, the show consistently ranked among the top 10 programs.

You Bet Your Life (NBC), 1950–1961. Host: Groucho Marx, Announcer: George Fenneman.

For all but two seasons of the show's eight-year run, Clayton Moore played the Masked Man with the horse named Silver and the Indian companion named Tonto.

The Lone Ranger

The Lone Ranger began as a radio show in 1933 and quickly became the most popular serial on the Mutual Broadcasting Network. ABC brought it to television in 1949, where it helped the network in its struggling early years by pulling in more viewers than any other ABC program until *Disneyland* came along in 1954.

The first TV episode, which was shown at least once during each season of the show's run, explained the origin of "the Masked Man," who was one of six Texas rangers ambushed by an outlaw gang. Five were killed and the sixth, John Reid, was left for dead. Reid crawled to a water hole, where an Indian named Tonto

discovered him. As the only survivor—the lone ranger—Reid donned a black mask to hide his identity and persuaded Tonto to help him track down the killers. They succeeded, then set out to help other victims across the West. It was during the debut program that Tonto first called his partner "Kemo sabe," meaning "trusty scout."

The show opened with a spoken introduction ("A fiery horse with the speed of light. . .") read over music from Rossini's "William Tell Overture." Most episodes ended with the hero's hearty call, "Hi-yo Silver, away!" as his horse galloped into the sunset after the duo had saved the day. Another trademark was the Lone Ranger's use of silver bullets, culled from a silver mine left to him by his brother, one of the deceased rangers. The silver mine provided him with money, too, since he refused to take gifts or money from those he helped.

Clayton Moore starred as the Lone Ranger for all but two seasons, and Jay Silverheels portrayed Tonto for the show's entire run. Moore and Silverheels were also paired in feature movies based on the series in the late 1950s.

The Lone Ranger (ABC), 1949–1957. The Lone Ranger: Clayton Moore (1949–1952, 1954–1957), John Hart (1952–1954), Tonto: Jay Silverheels.

The Man of Steel (George Reeves) is seen here with the series' first Lois Lane, Phyllis Coates.

The Adventures of Superman

Superman achieved multimedia success in the 1940s as the central character in comic books, a radio series, 30 movie serials, several feature-length cartoons, and, in 1951, a feature-length movie. That same year production started on a syndicated TV series, *The Adventures of Superman*, starring George Reeves as the Man of Steel and his human alter ego, mild-mannered reporter Clark Kent. Episodes of *The Adventures of Superman* first began airing in late 1952, and the show quickly became one of TV's most successful non-network productions.

Superman could fly "faster than a speeding bullet, leap tall buildings in a single bound," and "bend steel in his bare hands," to quote from each show's introduction. He also could split himself into two bodies, will himself through solid matter, and levitate objects. He had super breath, super hearing and super sight—including X-ray vision, microscopic vision, and telescopic vision. His only weakness was the mineral Kryptonite, found in pieces of green rock from his native planet, Krypton, which had exploded and sent fragments to Earth. If Superman came near Kryptonite, it sapped all of his strength. The first episode explained the character's background—how he was sent to Earth as an infant just before Krypton was destroyed, how he was found and adopted by a childless family named Kent who were aware of his background and his super powers, and how, as he grew up, he decided to use his powers to "fight a never-ending battle for truth, justice, and the American Way."

As Clark Kent, he went to work in Metropolis at the crusading newspaper, *The Daily Planet*. His colleagues included editor Perry White, ace reporter Lois Lane, and naive photographer Jimmy Olson. His co-workers often depended on Superman, but they never discovered Kent's true identity. The show ended in 1957. Two years later, actor Reeves was found dead of a gunshot wound. The coroner ruled it suicide, although the evidence has been challenged in recent years.

Superman (syndicated), 1952–1957. Superman/Clark Kent: George Reeves, Lois Lane: Phyllis Coates (1952), Noel Neill (1953-1957), Jimmy Olson: Jack Larson, Perry White: John Hamilton, Inspector William Henderson: Robert Shayne.

The second and more enduring Lois, Noel Neill, plays the intrepid reporter pecking out her story on a manual typewriter while Superman in his Clark Kent disguise looks on.

Veteran announcer Ralph Edwards created *This Is Your Life* as a radio series in 1948; it spent one year on CBS and another on NBC. In 1954, he revived the concept for NBC television, where it proved much more successful and durable.

The format was simple: the producers conspired to surprise an unsuspecting guest star with a recounting of his or her life. The subject was usually a celebrity, although the show occasionally spotlighted a person of merit outside of show business. Each show typically began with the guest having been lured by trick to the NBC studio or somewhere nearby. Edwards would then introduce himself, announcing "This is your life!" to the usually flabbergasted honoree. The guest would then be transported to the set and positioned on a couch while Edwards pulled out the *This Is Your Life* book of memoirs created specifically for him or her by the show's writers.

From there, Edwards would review the highlights of the guest's life. From time to time, his narrative would be punctuated by the offstage comments of individuals important to the honoree—relatives, teachers, early employers, childhood friends, and so forth. In each case, the guest would attempt to guess the identity of the speaker—often someone whom he or she had not seen in years—and then they would come together on stage for a hearty reunion. As might be expected, emotions often ran high. At the show's end, Edwards would present the guest with the book and usually some other keepsake.

This Is Your Life enjoyed its greatest success from 1953 to 1955. Its original run ended in 1961, and Edwards returned in the 1970s with a new, syndicated version.

This Is Your Life (NBC), 1952–1961. Host: Ralph Edwards.

Weekly for nine years, Ralph Edwards (standing) surprised celebrities with the stories of their public and private lives. Here the honoree is singer Dinah Shore, seated beside her then-husband, actor Robert Montgomery.

As the World Turns

As the World Turns and The Edge of Night became the first 30-minute weekday serials on April 2, 1956, the day both premiered on CBS-TV. Before then, such forerunners as Love of Life and Search for Tomorrow were limited to 15-minutes airings.

Already known as soap operas (because the sponsors were often makers of detergents and household cleansers), the daily serial format was established by such daytime radio programs as The Guiding Light in the 1940s. The most successful of them all in the late 1950s and through the 1960s was As the World Turns, created by legendary soap opera writer Irna Phillips.

Set in Oakdale, a fictional town in the Midwest, As the World Turns originally followed the diverse paths of the middle-class Hughes family and the upper-class Lowells. The Lowells' role quickly diminished, and the family eventually was written out of the series. The Hughes' offspring remain part of the action today.

At the outset, Helen Wagner played Nancy Hughes, remaining with the show until 1981. Don McLaughlin portrayed her husband, lawyer Chris Hughes; he was still an active cast member when he died in 1986 shortly following the show's 30th anniversary. Their children and grandchildren continue as characters today.

Eileen Fulton, as Lisa Miller, joined the cast in 1960 and ranks among daytime TV's most treacherous vixens. Among the regulars who moved on to greater fame over the years are Meg Ryan, Richard Thomas, Joyce Van Patten, Rebecca Holden, and Glynnis O'Connor.

As the World Turns (CBS), 1956– . (original cast) Chris Hughes: Don McLaughlin, Nancy Hughes: Helen Wagner, Don Hughes: Hal Studer, Penny Hughes: Rosemary Prinz, Bob Hughes: Bobby Alford, Grandpa Hughes: William Lee, Edith Hughes: Ruth Warrick, Jim Lowell: Les Damon, Claire Lowell: Anne Burr, Judge Lowell: William Johnstone, Ellen Lowell: Wendy Drew, Janice Turner Hughes: Joyce Van Patten, Dr. Doug Cassen: Nat Polen, Jeff Baker: Mark Rydell.

Seen here in 1957 are "Buffalo Bob" Smith, the creator of *Howdy Doody*, and the show's celebrated namesake. They are tacking up a wanted poster to announce their search for men and women who sat as kids in the Peanut Gallery during the show's first season in 1947.

WANTED

$100 REWARD

One Hundred Dollar reward for information leading to identification and location of the 8 children who were on original Howdy Doody Show December 27, 1947.

In case of ties or duplicate information, I will be the sole judge to determine the sharing of this reward.

SIGNED
Howdy Doody
NBC-TV
NEW YORK

Howdy Doody

Bob Smith, a one-time singer, came up with the phrase "Howdy doody" while hosting a children's program on a New York radio station. A character he created began introducing himself by exclaiming, "Well, howdy doody!" and the phrase caught on with the program's young listeners.

In 1947, Smith convinced NBC to televise a puppet show featuring a lead character named Howdy Doody. The network initially ran the show once a week as *Puppet Playhouse*, but its popularity led to airings three times a week and in August 1948, it started running daily, Monday through Friday.

The program took place in Doodyville, a town populated by circus characters and puppets. With an audience of children looking on from a set of bleachers known as the Peanut Gallery, Smith sang a song or two, introduced a short silent movie, and chatted with puppets about activities in Doodyville. By then, Smith was known as "Buffalo Bob," a name given him by a tribe of Sycapoose Indians living near Doodyville.

Smith's assistant and occasional antagonist was Clarabell, a silent clown played from 1947 to 1953 by Bob Keeshan, who later became TV's Captain Kangaroo. In addition to Howdy Doody, the show's cast of puppets included Phineas T. Bluster, mayor of Doodyville; Captain Scuttlebutt, a crusty old seaman; Double Doody, Howdy's twin brother; Heidi Doody, Howdy's sister; Flub-A-Dub, who consisted of parts from eight animals; Dilly Dally, a bumbling carpenter; and Gumby, a movable clay figure who was given his own series in 1957.

Howdy Doody was among the first series to be telecast in summer. It was also one of the first shows to be shown in color. NBC's owner, RCA, began experimenting with the process on *Howdy Doody* in the summer of 1953, and by September of 1955, all of the show's episodes were shown in color. The series continued to run weekdays until 1956, when it moved to Saturdays, where it remained until its cancellation four years later.

Howdy Doody (NBC), 1947–1960. Host: "Buffalo Bob" Smith, Clarabell: Bob Keeshan, Bobby Nicholson, Lew Anderson, Chief Thunderthud: Bill LeCornec, Princess Summerfall Winterspring: Judy Tyler, Linda Marsh, Bison Bill: Ted Brown, Ugly Sam: Dayton Allen.

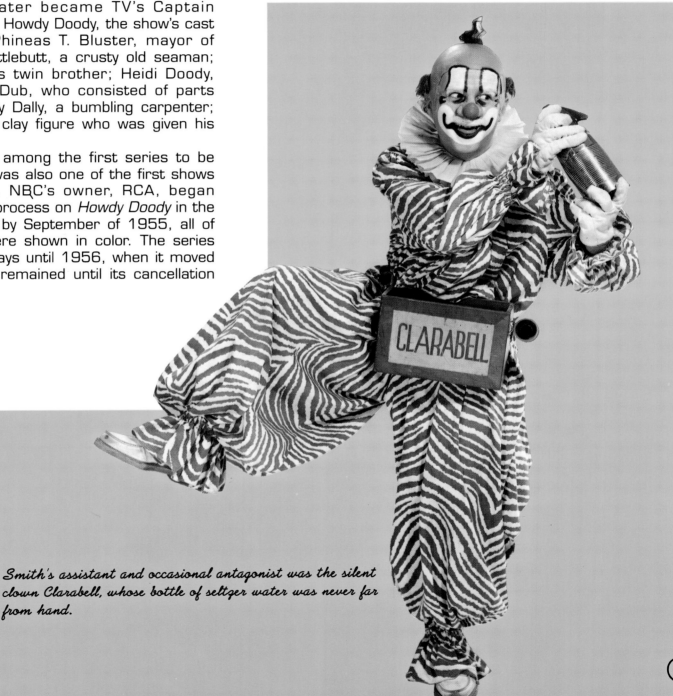

Smith's assistant and occasional antagonist was the silent clown Clarabell, whose bottle of seltzer water was never far from hand.

What's My Line was distinguished by its witty, intelligent moderator and panel, including (l. to r.) columnist Dorothy Kilgallen, publisher Bennett Cerf, and former actress Arlene Francis. The fourth panelist here is Hal Block, who served from 1950 to 1953. Moderator John Daly is standing.

MISS KILGALLEN   MR. CERF   MISS FRANCIS   MR. BLOCK

WHAT'S MY LINE?

Moderator Daly cracks up over the antics of "mystery guest" Eddie Cantor, who appeared on the show in January 1952.

What's My Line ranks as the longest-running game show in the history of prime-time television. The format was uncomplicated: a panel of four celebrities attempted to guess the occupation of a contestant by asking a series of questions, to which the contestant answered yes or no. For each negative response, the contestant won $50; 10 "no's" ended the game. Each show also featured a famous "mystery guest," with the panel donning blindfolds while the celebrity disguised his or her voice.

The program's charm came from the urbane wit of its host and panel members. John Daly, the series emcee throughout its 17-year run on CBS, had been an esteemed CBS radio news correspondent from 1937 to 1950, the year What's My Line began. In 1953, while hosting the game show, Daly was named anchorman of ABC Evening News, a post he held for seven years. The initial panel consisted of former New Jersey governor Harold Hoffman, Park Avenue psychiatrist Richard Hoffman, newspaper columnist Dorothy Kilgallen, and poet Louis Untermeyer. Only Kilgallen remained beyond the first year, staying until her death in 1965. Actress Arlene Francis joined the panel on the second telecast, and publisher Bennett Cerf joined in 1951. Both remained until the show's demise. Other regular panelists included gag writer Hal Block, comic Fred Allen, and the multi-talented Steve Allen, who first coined the famous saying, "Is it bigger than a breadbox?" during the program. From 1956 on, a celebrity guest panelist joined Cerf, Francis, and Kilgallen on the panel.

The series was the first success for producers Mark Goodson and Bill Todman, who went on to create *To Tell the Truth*, *I've Got a Secret*, *Match Game* and several other game shows.

What's My Line (CBS), 1950–1967. Host: John Daly. Panelists: Arlene Francis, Dorothy Kilgallen (1950–1965), Bennett Cerf (1951–1967), Hal Block (1950–1953), Fred Allen (1953–1956), Steve Allen (1953–1954).

Captain Kangaroo

Bob Keeshan's folksy, relaxed way endeared him to generations of youngsters, who knew him as the man with the huge jacket pockets—Captain Kangaroo.

ob Keeshan began entertaining children through television when he appeared as Clarabell on *Howdy Doody*. Then a New York station coaxed him into hosting two regional television programs, *Tinker's Workshop* and *Time for Fun*. CBS-TV noticed Keeshan's folksy, relaxed way with kids and hired him to host a weekday morning children's show called *Captain Kangaroo*. Named for Keeshan's character who boasted huge pockets on the front of his colorful jacket, *Captain Kangaroo* made its debut the same October day in 1955 as *The Mickey Mouse Club*. It went on to become the longest-running children's series on network television.

Keeshan ran the show with a calm tone and easy pace, his gentle manner informing each program. He addressed his skits directly to young viewers, and although he spoke with a childlike whimsy, he didn't come across as patronizing—as did the hosts of other children's programs. His primary sidekick was Mr. Green Jeans (Hugh Brannum), a farmer and amateur inventor who introduced animals and other topics pertaining to nature. Another regular was Dennis (Cosmo Allegretti), a clumsy assistant. Allegretti was also the program's puppeteer, creating the inquisitive Miss Frog, the brainy Wood Bird, the shy Bunny Rabbit, and the soft-spoken Mr. Whispers. Other human characters over the years included the health-conscious Slim Goodbody (John Burstein), Mr. Baxter (Larry Wall), and Debby (Debby Weems). Bill Cosby also appeared periodically in the show's final years.

In January 1956, the hour-long *Captain Kangaroo* expanded from five to six days a week to include Saturday mornings, a schedule the series maintained until 1968, when it was trimmed back to weekdays. In the fall of 1981, it was cut to 30 minutes and moved back an hour from its traditional 8 a.m. slot to allow for the expansion of the *CBS Morning News*. The show was moved to weekends in September 1982, marking the end of weekday network morning shows directed at children. It left the air in December 1984.

Captain Kangaroo (CBS), 1955–1984. Captain Kangaroo: Bob Keeshan, Mr. Green Jeans: Hugh Brannum, Dennis: Cosmo Allegretti, Slim Goodbody: John Burstein, Mr. Baxter: Larry Wall, Debby: Debby Weems, Bill Cosby: himself.

A daily highlight of Art Linkletter's House Party was the host's chat with a group of youngsters. Somehow Linkletter could always get the kids to say "the darndest things."

Art Linkletter's House Party

Art Linkletter was a familiar presence to radio listeners and television viewers throughout the 1950s, and his most popular program was his long-running daily program, *Art Linkletter's House Party*. Linkletter established the *House Party* format quickly when it began airing on CBS radio in 1944. The daily afternoon variety show featured the folksy, glib Linkletter engaging his audience with jokes, stunts, interviews, and contests. He'd encourage audience members to enact exploits from the silly to the outrageous for a chance at prizes. His most endearing feature was his daily interview with four young schoolchildren. He'd seat them on tall stools and coax humorous, candid comments from them. He later collected the interviews in several books, the first of which was titled *Kids Say the Darndest Things*.

Linkletter first appeared on TV as host of *Life with Linkletter* on ABC, a prime-time version of his successful daily *House Party* radio series, which aired from 1950 to 1952. That year, CBS grabbed him back and put him on the tube with *Art Linkletter's House Party*, which ran on weekday afternoons for 16 years. In 1968, the series was re-named *The Linkletter Show* and shifted to a morning time slot until it was canceled in 1969.

Linkletter also hosted a daily NBC program, *People Are Funny*, from 1954 to 1961.

Art Linkletter's House Party (CBS), 1952–1969. Host: Art Linkletter.

In 1954, Walt Disney did what no other Hollywood film studio head would have dreamed of doing—he became the host of his own television show. He is seen here introducing a future-oriented program called "Magic Highway, U. S. A."

Walt Disney's move into television production in 1954 is considered a landmark moment in television history. Until then, the major movie studios and leading film producers had boycotted the new entertainment medium, fearing its competition and criticizing its limitations. Disney changed that. In addition, Disney aligned himself with ABC-TV, boosting the struggling third network to major player status. *Disneyland* became ABC's first show to crack the Top 20 in Nielsen ratings. Moreover, if ABC hooked Disney by agreeing to invest in a California amusement park which would share the name of the series, that gamble paid off much better than the network expected. *Disneyland* was an anthology series that rotated nature stories, documentaries, adventure programs, and animated subjects. Its biggest initial splash came with a series of fictional episodes based on the true-life adventures of explorer Davy Crockett (Fess Parker). The three original Crockett programs ran on alternate weeks starting in December 1954. Even though Crockett was killed in the third episode, *Davy Crockett at the Alamo,* the public demand led Disney to create two more Crockett segments, from earlier portions of the westerner's life.

Among other popular programs were those focusing on nature and animals ("Sammy the Way Out Seal," "Ida the Offbeat Eagle"), documentaries hosted by Donald Duck or his uncle, Professor Ludwig Von Drake, and remakes of such classic tales as "Alice in Wonderland," "Babes in Toyland," and "Robin Hood."

The ABC series name was changed to *Walt Disney Presents* in 1958. Three years later, when the show transferred to NBC, it was called *Walt Disney's Wonderful World of Color*. In 1981, the program moved to CBS, thereby becoming the only prime-time series to have appeared on all three major networks. ABC picked up the show in 1986 after it had been off the air for three years, and in the fall of 1988, the series again switched titles and networks, turning up on NBC as *The Magical World of Disney*.

Disneyland (*Walt Disney Presents*) (ABC), 1954–1961. Host: Walt Disney.

The unexpected smash hit of _Disneyland_'s early years was "Davy Crockett," a five-episode series based on the life of the Indian fighter and U. S. congressman. Fess Parker (left) played Davy and Buddy Ebsen his sidekick, Georgie Russell.

Born Leonard Slye in Cincinnati, Ohio, Roy Rogers became known as the "King of the Cowboys," through a series of theatrical B Westerns and his weekly television show. His co-stars were his wife, Dale Evans, and his horse, Trigger.

Although Roy Rogers became known as "the King of the Cowboys," he actually grew up in Cincinnati, Ohio where he worked on a thoroughbred horse ranch as a teen-ager perfecting his riding skills. Born Leonard Slye, he migrated to California in 1930 at age 19, taking a job as a fruit picker before helping form a legendary western vocal group, the Sons of the Pioneers

By 1935, Rogers' boyish good looks and natural charm had landed him a few small roles in the movies. When Gene Autry left Republic Pictures in a dispute, Rogers was elevated to leading man and soon eclipsed Autry as the Western's top box-office star.

In the 1950s, as the popularity of cowboy movies waned, Rogers transferred to television with great success. His weekly prime-time series, *The Roy Rogers Show*, began in 1951 on NBC, co-starring his wife Dale Evans ("The Queen of the West") and bumbling sidekick Pat Brady.

The program allowed Rogers to successfully continue his movie image as a gentle, courageous crusader for law and order in the contemporary West. The trio resided at the Double R Bar Ranch with Roy's horse, Trigger, Dale's horse, Buttermilk, their German shepherd, Bullet, and Pat's broken-down jeep, Nellybelle. The Sons of the Pioneers were also on hand to harmonize during musical numbers with the stars, as in their theme song, "Happy Trails to You." The series ended in 1957.

The Roy Rogers Show (NBC), 1951–1957. Roy Rogers: himself, Dale Evans: herself, Pat Brady: himself, the Sons of the Pioneers.

News, Public
Affairs Programming,
and Special Events

3

The Army-McCarthy Hearings

In 1954, U.S. Senator Joseph McCarthy was stepping up his attacks on those American citizens whom he accused of sympathizing with the Communist party. The political practice known as redbaiting had grown through the early 1950s, when the Cold War and the threat of the atomic bomb had heightened paranoia among the populace. Feeding those fears were the loud accusations of the junior senator from Wisconsin, chairman of the Committee on Un-American Activities.

It was in early 1954 that McCarthy charged the communists with infiltrating the U.S. military and urged an investigation into the allegation. The Army-McCarthy Hearings began in late April and were telecast daily on ABC. An estimated 20 million people tuned in to see McCarthy recite his innuendos and crude, rambling tirades about "the Communist conspiracy." Representing the U.S. Army was Joseph Welch, the distinguished 63-year-old senior partner of a prestigious Boston law firm. A life-long Republican, he calmly refuted McCarthy's allegations with deliberate, fact-filled arguments.

Eventually, McCarthy turned on a young member of Welch's firm, charging him with being a member of the Lawyer's Guild, which McCarthy incorrectly described as "the legal bulwark for the Communist party." Welch stood and responded, saying "Until this moment, Senator, I think I never really gauged your cruelty or recklessness." The audience in the Senate meeting room cheered when Welch ended his comments.

The live hearings let people see the viciousness of McCarthy's unfounded attacks and his public support quickly subsided. In December, McCarthy was censured by both houses of Congress.

The Army-McCarthy Hearings (ABC), 1954.

The chief counsel for the Army was Joseph Welch, the distinguished 63-year-old senior partner of a prestigious Boston law firm, who calmly refuted McCarthy's allegations with deliberate, fact-filled arguments.

Many Americans got their first closeup view of Joseph McCarthy during the televised Army-McCarthy hearings in 1954. The snide innuendos and bullying tactics of the junior senator from Wisconsin did not sit well with viewers and he was censured by the Senate before the year's end.

(Page 51) Edward R. Murrow of See It Now.

The highlight of the pageant is, of course, the crowning of Miss America. On September 11, 1954, some 27 million television viewers watched as Evelyn Ay bestowed the honor upon Lee Ann Meriweather. Meriweather went on to become a TV actress, co-starring in *Barnaby Jones*.

The First Televised Miss America Pageant

The original Miss America Pageant took place in 1921 in Atlantic City, which has served as the venue for the annual event ever since. The winner was 16-year-old Margaret Gorman from Washington, D.C. Her talent was shooting marbles, and instead of a crown she received a three-foot statue of a golden mermaid.

She's come a long way, baby. The biggest change in the evolution of the Miss America Pageant occurred on September 11, 1954, when ABC presented a live, 90-minute telecast of the event and drew 27 million viewers, or 39 percent of the viewing audience.

ABC had considered telecasting the previous year, but withdrew when the pageant's director demanded that the show be blacked out in New Jersey and Philadelphia because of their proximity to the event itself. The director relented in 1954 when Philco signed on as sponsor and ABC contributed $10,000 to the pageant.

Miss America made a perfectly dramatic TV debut. In those years, the five finalists were kept offstage, coming out one by one as the runners-up were announced. Unknown to the contestants, ABC had placed a hidden camera backstage to capture their reactions.

One of the final two contestants was Lee Meriwether, a drama student at the City College of San Francisco and owner of a sharpshooter medal from the National Rifle Association. The program had already noted that her father had passed away a few weeks earlier. When she was declared Miss America, TV viewers saw her look skyward and say clearly, "You know I know how happy you are." She then cried throughout her victory walk.

The following season, Bert Parks took over as host and the pageant drew more than 40 percent of the TV audience. In 1957, when the program switched to CBS, more than 60 million people watched at home, and the pageant has remained an annual TV institution ever since.

Miss America Pageant (ABC), September 11, 1954. Host: Bob Russell.

Bert Parks became synonymous with the Miss America Pageant in the minds of many television viewers. He is seen here in his first appearance on the show in 1955 with the winner of that year's pageant, Sharon Ritchie.

Nixon's "Checkers" Speech

In the heat of the 1952 presidential campaign, reports began to surface that Republican vice-presidential candidate Richard M. Nixon had accepted $18,000 in donations to supplement his salary as a U. S. senator. As the allegations gained currency, Nixon's position as Dwight Eisenhower's running mate came under threat, with many Republicans around the country calling for his removal from the ticket. Even the presidential candidate, Dwight D. Eisenhower, was noncommittal in his support. Nixon, desperate to save his political career, decided to take his case to the American people.

With funding from the Republican National Committee, Nixon bought 30 minutes of prime time on all three networks on the night of September 22, 1952. His appeal drew an estimated 58 million viewers, the largest audience for a TV program at the time.

Nixon stood on a simple Los Angeles stage featuring a desk and a background of shelves lined with books, and he spoke without a script. He admitted the existence of the fund but emphasized that he had not used the money for himself and he had not provided special favors to the contributors. Every penny went to political expenses that he "did not think should be charged to taxpayers." He did not live extravagantly, he said. His wife owned not mink, but "a respectable Republican cloth coat."

The smears against him came from communist sympathizers, he claimed, and he expected them to continue. He even predicted he'd be attacked for accepting a gift from a Texas supporter, a cocker spaniel that his six-year-old daughter Tricia had named Checkers.

"The kids love that dog and I just want to say this right now . . . we're going to keep it," he said emotionally. He ended by asking people to telegraph the Republican National Committee to indicate whether he should stay or resign from the ticket.

Nearly two million Americans responded with wires of support, and another three million sent letters. A random selection of letters found only 39 negative responses out of 8,000. The speech, although full of inaccuracies and self-serving statements, immediately lifted Nixon's approval ratings among the American public. More importantly, it demonstrated the tremendous power of the medium in the electoral process, a power that has grown in significance ever since.

Richard Nixon Speech (all networks), September 23, 1952.

This photo of Richard Nixon on the campaign trail was taken two days after the vice-presidential candidate went on national television to dispute charges of financial improprieties.

The tag lines—"Good night, David," "Good night, Chet"— are among the best known in TV history. They were the sign-off of NBC's popular anchor team, Chet Huntley (left) and David Brinkley, who reported the news from their respective venues in New York and Washington, D. C.

The Huntley-Brinkley Report

NBC was the first network to develop the nightly newscast, running through various prototypes in the 1940s before hiring John Cameron Swayze as "anchorman" of the 15-minute *Camel News Caravan* in 1949.

In 1956, NBC decided to replace Swayze with anchors who had field experience in gathering news, choosing veterans Chet Huntley and David Brinkley and titled the weeknight telecast *The Huntley-Brinkley Report*. Huntley had worked in radio news since 1939 for CBS and ABC before joining NBC in 1955, two years after winning a prestigious Peabody Award for his reporting. Brinkley had experience as a wire-service journalist before joining NBC News in 1943. The two first worked as a team while covering political conventions for the 1956 presidential elections.

The anchors offered contrasting styles: Huntley, based in NBC's New York studios, was solemn and straightforward; Brinkley, reporting from a Washington bureau, was acerbic and opinionated. To establish warmth between the two, producer Reuven Frank suggested they close each program with "Good night, Chet . . . Good night, David." The exchange became a trademark, and the duo soon were TV's first celebrity news anchors, helping NBC remain the top-rated newscast until the late 1960s.

Huntley retired in 1970 and passed away four years later. Brinkley rotated the anchor spot with John Chancellor and Frank McGee for a year before Chancellor took over in 1971. Brinkley returned as his partner from 1976 to 1979.

The Huntley-Brinkley Report (NBC), 1956–1970.

After the first televised Academy Award presentations, business for the winning films soared. Thus, there was no studio opposition to the telecast the following year, when Audrey Hepburn, shown here, won as Best Actress for *Roman Holiday*. Note the several TV cameras and the monitors in the audience.

The Academy Awards' First Telecast

In 1953, the movie industry finally shook hands with its avowed enemy, television. Theater receipts had declined as TV's popularity had risen, and the movie studio heads initially refused to have anything to do with the upstart medium, strongly suggesting that their creative and technical people follow suit.

In 1953, however, the Academy of Motion Picture Arts and Sciences created a controversy by taking its annual awards gala to TV to celebrate its 25th anniversary. Three film studios withdrew financial support; others argued that putting the Oscars on the air would remind people of the quality of the top film productions and of the glamour and mystique of its leading stars. RCA contributed $100,000 to the academy to earn broadcasting rights for NBC.

The first telecast occurred on March 19, 1953, live from the Pantages Theater in Hollywood with a remote in New York, where Shirley Booth accepted the award for Best Actress for her role in *Come Back, Little Sheba*. A few traditions were established that

The winners for Best Actor and Actress on March 19, 1953, were Gary Cooper for *High Noon* and Shirley Booth for *Come Back, Little Sheba*.

The host of the first televised ceremonies was Bob Hope, who continued as emcee of the event for many years thereafter.

night: Bob Hope was the emcee, the speeches dragged on with endless thank yous, and the program ran over its time limit. For the one and only time, the network cut the festivities off, and thus viewers didn't see the Best Picture award go to *The Greatest Show on Earth*. Other winners included Gary Cooper for Best Actor in *High Noon* and John Ford as Best Director on *The Quiet Man*.

The first telecast was less polished than those of more recent vintage. There were no production numbers and no film clips accompanying awards announcements. The evening wear was decidedly less flashy, as all the potential winners had to have their dresses and suits approved by Edith Head, who served as guardian of hemlines and bodices for the network censors. Still, an estimated 40 million people watched the telecast, the largest audience for a commercial program on a single network at that point. *The Greatest Show on Earth,* which had ended its run, was rushed back into theaters, where it took in an additional $7.5 million at the box office. Business for *High Noon* and *Come Back, Little Sheba* increased by more than 300 percent. The studios, more than ever, understood the power of the tube, and never again have they objected to the inclusion of TV viewers at the festivities.

The Academy Awards (NBC), March 19, 1953. Master of Ceremonies: Bob Hope in Hollywood, Conrad Nagel in New York.

The show's first host was radio veteran Dave Garroway, whose relaxed manner fit the early time period. He is seen here giving his trademark sign-off, "Peace."

Joining the cast of <u>Today</u> in 1953 was a chimpanzee named J. Fred Muggs. He was joined two years later by Miss America, Lee Meriweather, who handled light features and fashion reports.

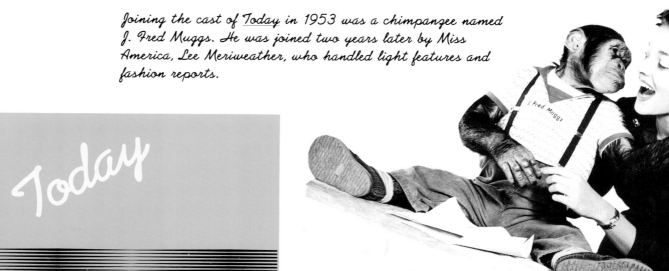

Today

Today introduced several important concepts to television: It was the first early morning program produced by a network, it was the first series designed to allow viewers to tune in without seeing the entire show, and it was the first targeted at people concurrently engaged in other activities, such as preparing for work or school.

The program—a mix of news, weather, interviews, and short feature stories—got off to a tentative start in January 1952, but became a profitable program in its second year. It now stands as network TV's longest-running weekday series.

The show's first host was radio veteran Dave Garroway, whose relaxed manner fit the early time period. Other regulars included Jack Lescoulie, who handled light features and sports, and Jim Fleming, who read the news. However, the biggest star of the initial years turned out to be J. Fred Muggs, a chimpanzee. When Muggs became a cast member in 1953, ratings shot up, mostly because youngsters tuned in to the program before school and brought their parents with them.

In the first of many on-air personnel changes over the years, newscaster Frank Blair replaced Fleming in 1953. He stayed on for 22 years. Garroway remained through the 1950s, leaving after the death of his second wife in 1961. Foreign correspondent John Chancellor then took over as host, lasting barely a year

in a job he hated. His replacement, Hugh Downs, proved more durable, heading the telecast until 1971. Barbara Walters joined during his tenure and was elevated to co-host in 1974.

Since then, there have been hosts who lasted, and those who didn't. Frank McGee and Jim Hartz suffered through short-term stints in the 1970s, and Chris Wallace and Deborah Norville met similar fates in the 1980s. More enduring hosts have included the teams of Tom Brokaw and Jane Pauley, then Pauley and Bryant Gumbel. Gene Shalit joined as movie reviewer in 1974, and Willard Scott came on as weatherman in 1980. The show celebrated its 40th anniversary in January 1992 with Gumbel and Katie Couric as co-hosts.

Today (NBC), 1952– . Hosts: Dave Garroway (1952-1961), John Chancellor (1961-1962), Hugh Downs (1962-1971), Frank McGee (1971-1974), Barbara Walters (1974-1976), Jim Hartz (1974-1976), Tom Brokaw (1976-1981), Jane Pauley (1976-1989), Bryant Gumbel (1982–), Chris Wallace (1982), Deborah Norville (1989-1991), Katie Couric (1991–).

For the first 15 years of the CBS nightly news program, its anchor was Douglas Edwards. During the 1950s, Edwards also hosted several entertainment programs, something his successors would avoid doing.

CBS Evening News

When CBS followed NBC's lead and initiated a 15-minute nightly newscast in 1948, the network chose Douglas Edwards as its anchor. A dry and authoritative news reader, the Oklahoma native began his broadcasting career with CBS radio in 1942, later anchoring the regional CBS news telecast in New York. For most of Edwards' 15 years with the TV program, it was known as *Douglas Edwards with the News*, but near the end of the 1950s the name became *CBS Evening News*.

The CBS news team made several important advances in the 1950s. In 1956, for instance, CBS became the first network to put the nightly telecast on videotape and air it at a later time slot in the western part of the country. Nevertheless, during its first decade, the show continually ranked behind the NBC news program, which featured the colorful styles of John Cameron Swayze and, starting in 1956, the anchor team of Chet Huntley and David Brinkley. CBS wouldn't step up to Number One in the ratings until the late 1960s when, during an era of turbulent news, America began turning to the comforting, reliable image of anchor Walter Cronkite.

Although CBS found its ratings success a long time in coming, it started fighting back before the end of Edwards' tenure. To provide news coverage of the 1960 Democratic and Republican presidential conventions, for example, it sent 25 reporters to the convention, under the direction of Cronkite, while Edwards anchored reports in the news studio in New York.

In addition to his news work, Edwards was host of and narrator for T*he Armstrong Circle Theater*, a live-drama series on CBS from 1957 to 1961. He was emcee for the short-lived *Masquerade Party* in 1953 and for the Sunday news program *F.Y.I.* in 1960.

After leaving the evening news show, Edwards continued to anchor a five-minute daily news program on CBS until April 1988. He also could be heard through the 1980s handling daily news reports on the CBS radio network.

CBS Evening News 1948-   . Anchor: Douglas Edwards (1948-1962).

Cinderella

Composer Richard Rodgers and lyricist Oscar Hammerstein II, famous for their successful Broadway musicals, certainly had a flair for dramatic timing. The two produced their first original television musical, a live telecast of *Cinderella* with Julie Andrews in the starring role, for CBS-TV on March 31, 1957. That day also marked the 14th anniversary of the opening performance of *Oklahoma!,* their first successful collaboration and the winner of the Pulitzer Prize.

Andrews was coming off of a grand Broadway triumph as the star of *My Fair Lady* when she presented the idea for a musical adaptation of *Cinderella* to CBS. The network liked the idea and asked Rodgers and Hammerstein if they would write it.

For the most part, the renowned duo remained faithful to the original fairy tale by the brothers Grimm. Andrews plays a young, sweet scrubwoman who is treated with scorn by her wealthy stepmother and stepsisters. However, on a night when she's left behind while the others head off for a royal ball, her life becomes enchanted thanks to a fairy godmother, a pumpkin coach, a glass slipper, and Prince Charming (Jon Cypher).

Rodgers and Hammerstein do take a few liberties. They give the prince a pair of comic parents, and they lighten up the stepmother (Ilka Chase) and stepsisters (Alice Ghostley and Kaye Ballard), who appear more pompous and silly than cruel and evil.

Cinderella (CBS), March 31, 1957. Cinderella: Julie Andrews, Prince Charming: Jon Cypher, Stepmother: Ilka Chase, Stepsisters: Alice Ghostley, Kaye Ballard.

Fresh from her Broadway triumph as Eliza Doolitle in My Fair Lady, Julie Andrews enchanted television viewers on March 31, 1957, playing Cinderella in a live version of the fairy tale with a score by Rodgers and Hammerstein.

One of *See It Now*'s most distinguished episodes, broadcast in December 1952, took Murrow to South Korea, where he interviewed soldiers fighting in the trenches of the Korean War.

See It Now

ee It Now was television's first high-quality, in-depth documentary program, and its host Edward R. Murrow was broadcast journalism's most revered figure. *See It Now* is considered Murrow's most significant offering, and he won five Emmy Awards in the 1950s because of it.

Murrow joined CBS in 1935, helping forge the network's news division and played a leading role in establishing broadcasting as a credible news forum, first with his dramatic live radio reports from Europe during World War II and later with his TV reports on *See It Now*. The latter program began as a Sunday afternoon show in 1953, with the debut featuring the first live coast-to-coast transmission by a network series.

Although *See It Now* contained its lighter moments, such as Murrow's interview with painter Grandma Moses, its reputation rested on its tendency to tackle important political and social controversies with unflinching directness. The show's most acclaimed subject was a three-part exposé of the unethical tactics of Senator Joseph McCarthy of Wisconsin, a report that helped end the senator's career and with it the red-scare witch-hunt known as McCarthyism. Other distinguished episodes included an interview with atomic scientist J. Robert Oppenheimer and his misgivings about the nuclear technology he helped create; a Christmas broadcast featuring soldiers in the trenches in Korea; stories on Africa and the Middle East; a ground-breaking report on the link between cancer and cigarette smoking; and a 1954 program on the Supreme Court's historic desegregation decision.

Six months after its premiere, *See It Now* moved to a prime-time slot, where it remained for three years. In 1955, the show began running as a series of periodic hour-long specials. The last *See It Now* was aired in July 1958. Ten years later, the show's director, Don Hewitt, helped create *60 Minutes*, a

Broadcast journalism's most revered figure was Edward R. Murrow and See It Now his most significant offering. He won five Emmy Awards for the documentary program.

program inspired by Murrow's work. Hewitt remains the successful news magazine's executive producer.

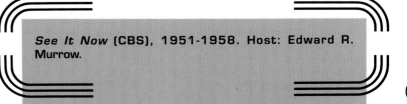

See It Now (CBS), 1951-1958. Host: Edward R. Murrow.

Meet The Press

Meet the Press, the longest-running series in television history, was created in 1945 as a public affairs program for NBC radio by free-lance journalist Martha Rountree and magazine publisher and editor Lawrence Spivak. Two years later, NBC turned it into a 30-minute, prime-time program with Rountree continuing as moderator and Spivak as a panelist.

Billed as "America's Press Conference of the Air," the setting and format has remained consistent through the decades: the show has always emanated from an NBC studio in Washington, D.C., and it has always featured a panel of journalists questioning a political figure or figures. At one time or another, nearly every American official of note has appeared on the program, as have many foreign diplomats.

In the summer of 1951, *Meet the Press* ran twice a week in prime time. Two years later, Spivak bought out Rountree's interest in the program, and Ned Brooks took over as moderator, with Spivak staying on as panelist and occasional moderator. In 1965, Spivak began a 10-year stint as moderator as *Meet the Press* moved from prime time to its present position on Sunday afternoons. For his final program, Spivak's guest was President Gerald Ford, the only time an incumbent chief executive has appeared on the show. As the years have passed, Spivak has been succeeded by newsmen Bill Monroe, Marvin Kalb, Chris Wallace, and Garrick Utley.

Meet the Press (NBC), 1947– . Moderators: Martha Rountree, Ned Brooks, Lawrence Spivak, Bill Monroe, Marvin Kalb, Chris Wallace, Garrick Utley.

The co-creator and long-time moderator of <u>Meet the Press</u> was Lawrence Spivak (right). He is seen here in a publicity photo for a program that featured former president Herbert Hoover as the guest.

Anthologies and Dramatic Series

4

In 1959, Bob Cummings took time out from his own sitcom, _Love that Bob_, to appear in the Rod Serling drama, "Bomber's Moon," in which he played a ruthless air force pilot during World War II. Seen with him here are Hazel Court and Pat O'Malley.

(Previous page) Raymond Burr as defense attorney Perry Mason in _Perry Mason_.

Playhouse 90, perhaps the most ambitious series ever presented on television, is considered among the crowning achievements of the medium's "Golden Age."

For its debut season on CBS in 1956, principal director John Frankenheimer was faced with the challenge of presenting a high-quality, 90-minute live drama once a week. To pull it off was akin to staging a complex military maneuver: the actors' movements had to be exactly executed, the timing precisely maintained, and the camera angles perfectly set. A mistake could spell disaster for the entire production in front of millions of viewers.

The premiere featured an original drama by Rod Serling, entitled "Forbidden Area," starring Charlton Heston, Tab Hunter, and Vincent Price. The second show, which ranks among TV's most renowned productions, was "Requiem for a Heavyweight," another Serling original, starring Jack Palance as a down-and-out boxer. Other highly acclaimed episodes included "The Miracle Worker," "Charley's Aunt," "The Days of Wine and Roses," "Heart of Darkness," "Judgment at Nuremberg," and a two-part adaptation of "For Whom the Bell Tolls."

By the second season, the producers were allowed to film about one of every four dramas, relieving some of the weekly pressure. The 1958 season saw the introduction of videotape and after that the thrills and perils of live broadcasts vanished for the most part. For the fourth and final season, the show adopted an alternate-week schedule, sharing its time period with a variety show called _The Big Party_.

Playhouse 90 (CBS), 1956–1960.

Playhouse 90

One of the most celebrated productions in the distinguished history of _Playhouse 90_ was "Requiem for a Heavyweight," Rod Serling's tale of a down-and-out boxer, starring Jack Palance. The show also featured Keenan Wynn (left) and his father, Ed.

In Wagon Train, veteran film actor Ward Bond (right) revived his role as Maj. Seth Adams from the 1950 movie, _Wagonmaster_. His chief scout was the dashing Flint McCullough, played by Robert Horton.

Cast changes in the series after Bond's death and Horton's departure saw John McIntire (second from left) become wagonmaster Chris Hale and Scott Miller (right) as scout Duke Shannon. Other regulars included Terry Wilson (left) as ramrod Bill Hawks and Frank McGrath (second from right) as cook Charlie Wooster.

Wagon Train

Based on the pioneering legends of the post–Civil War era, *Wagon Train* was a Western constantly on the move. At the start of each season, the *Wagon Train* crew set off from St. Joseph, Missouri heading west across the violent Great Plains, the rugged Rocky Mountains and the punishing deserts. By spring, the wagons reached California—just in time for the end of the TV season.

The show, which began on NBC in 1957, was based on a popular 1950 movie, *Wagonmaster*, starring Ward Bond. Bond revived his role as Major Seth Adams in the TV series, heading a large cast until his death midway through the 1960 season. In 1961, John McIntire was introduced as the new wagonmaster, Chris Hale. He held the post until the show's demise in 1965. Robert Horton played the hardy scout Flint McCullough, until he left in 1962, saying he had tired of working in Westerns. He was replaced by Scott Miller as scout Duke Shannon, who was joined a few years later by TV-Western veteran Robert Fuller.

More than any other Western, *Wagon Train* made effective use of its weekly guest stars. The scripts were often character studies of the God-fearing settlers, the marauding outlaws, the con men, and the adventurers that made up the train or that the travelers encountered on the way west.

In its first season, *Wagon Train* went head-to-head on Wednesday nights with *I Love Lucy*, which had been the top-rated show for four of the five previous years. *Wagon Train* won out, ranking 23rd for the 1957–1958 season while *I Love Lucy* dropped out of the top 25. Lucy and Desi moved time slots the following year, and *Wagon Train* jumped up to number two behind *Gunsmoke*. It remained number two for three seasons, then overtook its competitor to become TV's top-rated show in 1961. The next year,

Wagon Train moved to ABC and slipped to number 25. ABC moved it to Tuesdays in 1963 and expanded it to 90 minutes; its popularity further decreased. It was canceled after the 1964/65 season.

Wagon Train (NBC), 1957–1962; (ABC), 1962–1965. Major Seth Adams: Ward Bond (1957–1961), Flint McCullough: Robert Horton (1957–1962), Bill Hawks: Terry Wilson, Charlie Wooster: Frank McGrath, Duke Shannon: Scott Miller (1961–1964), Christopher Hale: John McIntire (1961–1965), Barnaby West: Michael Burns (1963–1965), Cooper Smith: Robert Fuller (1964–1965).

Wagon Train told the fictional stories of those who trekked west and the people they encountered along the way. Seen here in "The Mary Halstead Story" is Agnes Moorehead who made the journey to find her long-lost son, played by Tom Pittman.

D ragnet began airing on NBC in January 1952 after three years as a successful radio show. At the time, TV's handful of detectives tended to be romantic rogues (*Man Against Crime, Martin Kaye, Private Eye*) or effete, intellectual clue trackers (*Ellery Queen, Mark Saber*).

As one of the first reality-based drama series, *Dragnet* changed the tone of the television drama. The show was produced and directed by lead actor Jack Webb, a successful movie star who admired nuts-and-bolts police work. Webb played Sergeant Joe Friday, badge No. 714 for the Los Angeles Police Department, who was dedicated to the deliberate pursuit of routine crime detection. Friday's partner changed often in the early years until Ben Alexander, as Officer Frank Smith, signed on in 1953.

Friday's voice provided the no-nonsense narration, which closely adhered to a time line—"9:15 a.m. We were assigned a homicide case that came in that morning." The stories were drawn from the files of the LAPD, and the segments followed Friday and his partner as they unglamourously tracked their leads.

Friday's style was soldierly and impassive. He'd introduce himself with a flat "Name's Friday, I'm a cop," and when witnesses or victims veered into embellishment, he'd rein them in with "Just the facts, ma'am (or sir)."

At the end of the show, an announcer would emphasize the show's serious nature by ominously stating: "The story you have just seen is true. The names have been changed to protect the innocent." Then, after a commercial, the announcer would reveal the outcome of the accused's trial and the severity of his or her sentence as he or she stood as if posing for a police blotter.

Dragnet ranked among TV's five most popular series from 1952 to 1955. It remained in the Top 20 until 1957 and was canceled two years later. Webb

revived his role and the series in 1967 for a three-year run with Harry Morgan as his new partner, Officer Bill Gannon. A comic spoof of *Dragnet* was released as a feature film in 1987 with Dan Ackroyd as Friday's clone-like nephew and Tom Hanks as his partner.

Dragnet (NBC), 1952–1959, 1967-1970. Sergeant Joe Friday: Jack Webb, Sergeant Ben Romero: Barton Yarborough (1951), Sergeant Ed Jacobs: Barney Phillips (1952), Officer Frank Smith: Herb Ellis (1952), Ben Alexander (1953–1959), Officer Bill Gannon: Harry Morgan (1967–1970).

In an era of larger-than-life TV detectives, Dragnet featured a nuts-and-bolts cop named Joe Friday (right), played by Jack Webb. For this Los Angeles detective, seen here at a crime scene with partner Officer Frank Smith (Ben Alexander), "just the facts" were enough.

Granite-faced Robert Stack brought no-nonsense conviction to the role of Eliot Ness, the real-life U.S. treasury agent who helped thwart organized crime in 1930s Chicago. In 1991, 28 years after the series ended, Stack reprised the role in a made-for-TV movie.

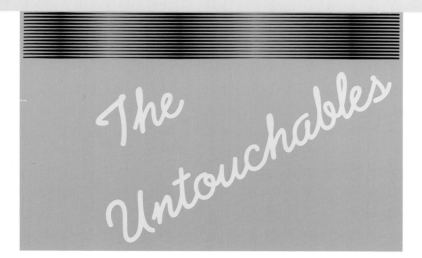

The Untouchables

The Untouchables, when introduced by ABC in 1959, became one of TV's most controversial series. Public officials blasted the gratuitous violence—every episode featured a few victims riddled by machine guns, mowed down by a speeding black sedan, or hung in a meat locker. Italian-American groups objected to the obvious ethnicity of the criminals. The FBI took issue with its historical accuracy. Law officers protested the occasional depiction of crooked cops. And prison directors disliked the suggestion that some hoodlums received preferential treatment behind bars.

The series was inspired by the real-life exploits of U.S. treasury agent Eliot Ness, who had helped end gangster Al Capone's reign of terror in Chicago in the 1930s. The success of a *Desilu Playhouse* dramatization of the Capone-Ness story on CBS in April 1959 led to the ABC series that fall. The title came from the name a Chicago newspaper had given to the band of ethical federal agents. But the series took great license in portraying them, especially in their captures of well-known underworld figures other than Capone.

The program was narrated by journalist Walter Winchell and produced by Quinn Martin, who went on to use a similar narrative style in *The F. B. I.*, *The Fugitive*, and *The Invaders*. In the lead as Eliot Ness was Robert Stack, who accepted the role after Van Johnson and Van Heflin turned it down. Stack, who had appeared in movies throughout the 1940s, including *The High and the Mighty* and *Written on the Wind,* had embraced TV with gusto, having appeared in several dramatic anthologies before landing the Ness role.

In addition to its regulars, *The Untouchables* offered a showcase for the talents of several notable guest actors. James Caan made his first major TV appearance on the show in 1962, and Robert Redford appeared in 1963. Barbara Stanwyck took on a recurring role that same year.

By its second season, *The Untouchables* was TV's eighth-rated show. The next year, ABC moved the 60-minute program to a later Thursday night slot, and it slipped in the ratings. A move to Tuesday in 1962 didn't help, and the show was canceled in 1963.

In 1987, a successful movie loosely based on the series was released with actor Kevin Costner starring as Ness.

The Untouchables (ABC), 1959–1963. Eliot Ness: Robert Stack, Agent Martin Flaherty: Jerry Paris (1959–1960), Agent William Youngfellow: Abel Fernandez, Agent Enrico Rossi: Nick Georgiade, Frank Nitti: Bruce Gordon.

The Hallmark Hall of Fame

switched from plays to original made-for-TV movies, but the work remained superb.

The dramas were televised exclusively on NBC until 1979. Subsequent productions have been shown on other networks, including CBS, ABC, and PBS, as well as NBC.

The Hallmark Hall of Fame (NBC), 1952–1955. Host: Sarah Churchill.

The Hallmark Hall of Fame is the lone survivor of the wealth of dramatic anthologies presented during the early days of television. Ironically, the *Hall of Fame* wasn't among the highest-profile dramas of the time. It served primarily as a summer replacement show from 1952 to 1955 and followed the better-known, more prolific *Philco-Goodyear Television Playhouse* on Sunday nights.

Nonetheless, like the other anthologies, *The Hallmark Hall of Fame* offered top-flight, theatrical quality television, with presentations ranging from such classics as *Hamlet*, *Moby Dick*, and *A Doll's House* to such newer works as Noel Coward's *A Brief Encounter* and James Costigan's *Little Man of Alban*. The casts included some of the most revered stage actors of the period, among them Dame Judith Anderson, Richard Burton, Dirk Bogarde, Orson Welles, Alfred Lunt, Alec Guinness, Ralph Richardson, and Julie Harris. The artistic merit of these dramas produced by the Hallmark Card Company and other corporate sponsors led critics to refer to the medium's early years as "The Golden Age of Television."

From 1956 until the end of the decade, Hallmark continued to present *Hall of Fame* productions at a rate of about five or six a year. In the 1960s and 1970s, the production schedule slowed and the focus

A veteran of numerous Hallmark Hall of Fame productions was Julie Harris, seen here as Joan of Arc in The Lark, which aired in February 1957.

In April 1959, Hallmark Hall of Fame featured a 90-minute version of Eugene O'Neill's comedy, Ah, Wilderness! with a cast that included (l. to r.) Lloyd Nolan as Nat Miller; Helen Hayes as his wife, Essie; Burgess Meredith as Uncle Sid; and Betty Field as Aunt Lily.

For 14 seasons *Bonanza* related the adventures of the Cartwrights, a father and three sons living on a one thousand-square-mile ranch in the Old West. Standing are (l. to r.) Michael Landon as Little Joe; Dan Blocker as Hoss; and Lorne Green as Ben, the patriarch of the clan. Pernell Roberts as the eldest son, Adam, is seated.

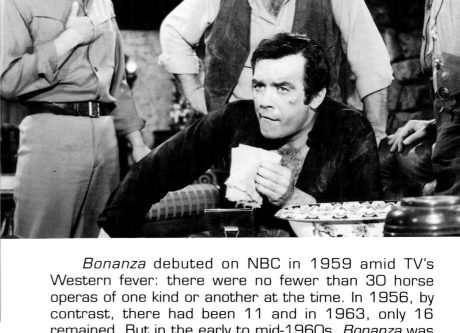

Bonanza

Bonanza civilized the Western drama. The central character wasn't a lawman or a heroic drifter, and gunfights were rare. Instead, the stories focused on the relationships of a hardworking widower and his three sons in the Old West.

The members of the Cartwright family were independent, honorable, caring, and humorous. They lived on a sprawling ranch called the Ponderosa, named for the type of pine that spread across its one thousand square miles.

Ben Cartwright (Lorne Greene) was TV's ultimate father figure, firm yet understanding and loving. His eldest son, Adam (Pernell Roberts), was intelligent, sensitive, and slow to anger; Hoss (Dan Blocker), the middle son, was a gentle, naive giant, eager to please and easy to dupe; and Little Joe (Michael Landon) was an impetuous youngster who never quite matured and whose impulsiveness continually landed him in fights and questionable affairs. Ben's sons bore diverse looks and personalities because each had been born of a different mother. The women were deceased, and their stories were told in flashbacks.

Bonanza debuted on NBC in 1959 amid TV's Western fever: there were no fewer than 30 horse operas of one kind or another at the time. In 1956, by contrast, there had been 11 and in 1963, only 16 remained. But in the early to mid-1960s, *Bonanza* was in its glory, ranking as the top-rated series from 1964 to 1967 and among the top four programs from 1961 to 1970. Pernell Roberts left the show in 1965, leaving two brothers on the ranch. Then, in 1972, Dan Blocker died suddenly. The show was canceled in January 1973.

Bonanza (NBC), 1959–1973. Ben Cartwright: Lorne Greene, Little Joe Cartwright: Michael Landon, Eric "Hoss" Cartwright: Dan Blocker (1959–1972), Adam Cartwright: Pernell Roberts (1959–1965), Hop Sing: Victor Sen Yung, Sheriff Roy Coffee: Ray Teal (1961–1971), Candy: David Canary (1967–1970, 1972–1973), Griff King: Tim Matheson (1972–1973).

The biggest star to emerge from *Bonanza* was Michael Landon, who went on to produce and star in two other long-running series, *Little House on the Prairie* and *Highway to Heaven*, before his untimely death in 1991.

Award-winning writer Rod Serling became best known to TV fans for his pointed comments at the opening and closing of each episode of The Twilight Zone. Serling also produced the series and wrote more than half of the episodes.

The Twilight Zone

In the early 1950s, playwright Rod Serling was a prolific contributor to TV's live-drama anthology series, winning Emmy Awards for writing "Patterns" for *Kraft Television Theater* and "Requiem for a Heavyweight" and "The Comedian" for *Playhouse 90*.

But Serling will be remembered more for his work on *The Twilight Zone*, a science-fiction anthology series which he created, produced, and introduced each week with a distinctive monologue suggesting "there is a fifth dimension beyond that which is known to man. . . . This is the dimension of imagination. It is an area we call the Twilight Zone."

Serling wrote 89 of the 151 episodes, most of which featured well-developed, offbeat plots with moralistic twists. Fans of the series usually rattle off favorite episodes. Among the most frequently mentioned are "Nightmare at 20,000 Feet" with William Shatner, "The Hitchhiker" with Inger Stevens, "Time Enough to Last" with Burgess Meredith, "Where Is Everybody?" with Earl Holliman, "The Dummy" with Cliff Robertson, "Nothing in the Dark" with Robert Redford, and "Escape Clause" with David Wayne.

The Twilight Zone debuted on CBS in October 1959, and the 30-minute episodes ran for three years. After a year's absence, public outcry was so great that in 1963 CBS brought back *The Twilight Zone* in an hour-long format. It rolled back to a half-hour for its next and last season.

The Twilight Zone (CBS), 1959–1964. Host: Rod Serling.

In "One for the Angels," comic actor Ed Wynn took on the dramatic role of a small-time pitchman who appeals to Death for the life of a dying child.

One of the classic episodes of the series, "Nightmare at 20,000 Feet," starred William Shatner as a man afraid of air travel. It was remade for the 1983 theatrical film, _Twilight Zone—The Movie_, with John Lithgow in the Shatner role.

The 30-minute dramatic series, Sea Hunt, featured Lloyd Bridges as Mike Nelson, an ex-Navy frogman whose business involved underwater investigations.

Sea Hunt

When producer Ivan Tors first proposed a series centered around an underwater adventurer, the three networks turned it down, saying the show would be too expensive to produce and the submerged setting too restrictive to scriptwriters. So Tors took it to television syndicator Frederic W. Ziv, who began selling *Sea Hunt* to network affiliates and independent stations. The show proved to be an immediate hit, staying in production from 1957 through 1961.

Sea Hunt featured actor Lloyd Bridges as expert skin-diver Mike Nelson, an ex-Navy frogman whose business involved underwater investigations. His work ranged from retrieving sunken goods to dramatic deep-sea rescues to U.S. security missions, and a majority of the 30-minute programs took place underwater or on Nelson's boat, the *Argonaut*.

Indeed, the show did prove costly and difficult to create. Filming had to follow the warm water from California to Florida to the Caribbean, and most of the work was done at depths of 20 to 40 feet. The crew included a number of diving and underwater experts, including ex-frogman Jon Lindbergh (son of aviator Charles Lindbergh) and an underwater photography specialist, Lamar Boren.

Bridges was the only regular cast member. Prior to *Sea Hunt*, the former college athlete had appeared on TV in several live dramas and anthologies; afterward, he was a leading small-screen presence, starring in several other series, including *Joe Forrester*, *The Loner*, *San Francisco International Airport*, and *Paper Dolls*, and making guest appearances in *Police Story* and *Roots* among others. He also appeared occasionally in films, such as *Airplane*, but left most of the silver screen work to his sons Beau (who had gotten an early start in several *Sea Hunt* episodes) and Jeff.

Sea Hunt was revived briefly in 1987 with Ron Ely (formerly TV's Tarzan) in the Mike Nelson role. The syndicated show lasted only a few weeks.

Sea Hunt (syndicated), 1957–1961. Mike Nelson: Lloyd Bridges.

Maverick

Although brothers Bret and Bart Maverick (James Garner, top, and Jack Kelly) preferred gambling and female companionship to gunplay, trouble always seemed to find them. Most episodes featured one brother or the other, but occasionally, as here, the duo appeared together.

Maverick started in 1957 as a straightforward Western about a dapper card player in the Old West. But, after several episodes, a crafty scriptwriter slipped in a few satirical lines, allowing James Garner (as Bret Maverick) to display his comic ability effectively. By mid-season, *Maverick* had become as much comedy as drama.

Bret Maverick was everything other Western heroes weren't: A con man with a knack for cards and gambling, a ladies' man with a sardonic sense of humor, an inept gunman with a cowardly streak who preferred avoiding confrontations.

At first, Garner was to be the series' only star. When first-year production ran behind schedule, however, ABC introduced a second devious Maverick, Bret's brother Bart (Jack Kelly). The two rarely appeared together: about one-third of the first year's shows featured Bart, the rest focused on Bret. But, by 1960, the two were evenly split. Garner quit in a contract dispute that year, and Kelly starred in virtually all of the final shows, though a third brother, Brent Maverick (Robert Colbert, who not coincidentally resembled Garner) was introduced. The ratings declined after Garner's departure, and the show ended in 1962.

Its cast was small but illustrious. Besides Garner and Kelly, the show featured Roger Moore, later *The Saint* and James Bond, as English cousin Beau Maverick from 1960–1962, and Efrem Zimbalist, Jr. (*The F. B. I.*) and Richard Long (*Big Valley*) had recurring roles.

Among the best-known episodes were parodies of other leading television programs. An episode named "Gunshy" poked fun at *Gunsmoke*, another lampooned *Dragnet* with Garner providing deadpan narration in the style of Sgt. Joe Friday. Then there was the *Bonanza* takeoff featuring ranching baron Joe

Wheelright trying to find wives for his three dim-witted sons—Moose, Small Paul, and Henry.

In 1979, CBS created *Young Maverick*, featuring Charles Frank as Ben Maverick, the Harvard-educated cousin of Bret and Bart. It lasted only two months. In 1981, Garner revived his role in *Bret Maverick*, but somehow the old magic was missing and NBC canceled the series after its first season.

Maverick (ABC), 1957–1962. Bret Maverick: James Garner (1957–1960), Bart Maverick: Jack Kelly (1957–1962), Samantha Crawford: Diane Brewster (1958–1959), Cousin Beauregard Maverick: Roger Moore (1960–1961), Brent Maverick: Robert Colbert (1961).

Before making the film version of No Time For Sergeants, Andy Griffith (right) brought his Broadway hit to The U. S. Steel Hour. The small-screen adaptation aired in March 1955.

Veteran comic actor Bert Lahr, best known as the Lion in the 1939 film, The Wizard of Oz, starred in "You Can't Win," which aired on The U. S. Steel Hour in November 1957.

The U. S. Steel

Hour

The U. S. Steel Co. began sponsoring a live dramatic anthology series on ABC radio in 1945 with assistance from the Theater Guild, an organization of actors, directors, dramatists, and others. Originally called *Theater Guild on the Air*, the series was designed to showcase first-rate New York plays featuring distinguished casts.

In 1953, the Guild persuaded U. S. Steel to produce a similar live program for television. The ABC premiere of *The U. S. Steel Hour* featured Broadway veterans Gary Merrill and Richard Kiley in the tensely dramatic *P.O.W.* Other presentations included Tallulah Bankhead in *Hedda Gabler*; Andy Griffith in the original

No Time for Sergeants; Paul Newman and George Peppard in the original *Bang the Drum Slowly*; Cliff Robertson in *The Two Worlds of Charlie Gordon*, which later became the movie *Charley* and won Robertson an Academy Award for Best Actor; Edward Mulhare in *The Importance of Being Earnest*; and a Duke Ellington musical narrative, *A Drum Is a Woman*.

The program aired on alternate weeks for 10 years, during which more than 200 live plays were presented. It moved from ABC to CBS in 1955, sharing its Wednesday time slot with its former competitor, *The Armstrong Circle Theater*.

The U. S. Steel Hour (ABC), 1953–1955; (CBS), 1955–1963.

"Bang the Drum Slowly" was the story of a hotshot pitcher and his dim-witted catcher. Later made into a film with Michael Moriarty and Robert De Niro, The U. S. Steel Hour version starred (l. to r.) Paul Newman, George Peppard, and Albert Salmi.

The intrepid marshal of Dodge City, Kansas was Matt Dillon, played throughout the show's 20-year run by James Arness. CBS initially offered the role to John Wayne, who turned it down, recommending his six-foot-seven-inch friend instead.

The leading players of Gunsmoke were largely unknown to television viewers when the series debuted in 1955, but they became familiar faces during the show's long run. They were (l. to r.) Milburn Stone as Doc Adams, Dennis Weaver as Chester Goode, and Amanda Blake as Kitty Russell.

Gunsmoke

*G*unsmoke began as a CBS radio program in 1952 with William Conrad (later TV's *Cannon*) as the stern voice of Marshal Matt Dillon. When CBS created a TV version in 1955, the network's first choice for the starring role was John Wayne, who turned it down, recommending instead his friend, the six-foot-seven-inch James Arness. (Wayne introduced the debut program, describing it as a new kind of Western that was more realistic than previous serial shoot-em-ups.)

Arness played the imperfect Dillon to perfection. The early shows opened with the marshal in a quick-draw showdown on Main Street in Dodge City, Kansas. The outlaw fired faster, but missed. Dillon was slower, but his aim was true. Over the years, his character grew to be a wise, rugged lawman who represented prairie justice and morality.

Arness led TV's largest, most durable cast. Milburn Stone spent 20 years as the craggy, sympathetic Doc Adams. Amanda Blake lasted 19 years as the hard-shelled, soft-hearted Miss Kitty Russell, owner of the Long Branch Saloon. Dennis Weaver was the limping, timid deputy Chester P. Goode. His 1964 departure led to scruffy Festus Haggen's appointment as deputy and elevated the actor who played him, Ken Curtis, from bit player to supporting lead. Burt Reynolds also starred as the rugged half-Indian Quint Asper from 1962–1965.

Originally a 30-minute show on Saturday nights, *Gunsmoke* helped create TV's obsession with the Western and then outlived all of the others. By its third season, it had grown into TV's number one show, staying there from 1957–1961. It expanded to an hour in 1961 and then went into decline in the mid-1960s. CBS was set to cancel the series when chairman William Paley suggested a move to Mondays. The show staged a huge comeback in its new time slot and lasted until 1975, when the era of the TV Western ended. Arness re-enacted his Dillon role in made-for-TV movies in 1986, 1990, and 1991.

Gunsmoke (CBS), 1955–1975. (principals) Marshal Matt Dillon: James Arness, Dr. Galen (Doc) Adams: Milburn Stone, Kitty Russell: Amanda Blake (1955–1974), Chester Goode: Dennis Weaver (1955–1964), Quint Asper: Burt Reynolds (1962–1965), Festus Haggen: Ken Curtis (1964–1975).

The Millionaire

Eccentric multibillionaire John Beresford Tipton was a philosophical fellow intrigued with how people handled newfound wealth. As the unseen central character of the weekly CBS dramatic series *The Millionaire*, he would send a cashier's check for a million tax-free dollars to some unsuspecting person he had never met. The series then portrayed how this gift changed the lives of the recipient and those who knew him or her, thereby providing a different answer each week to the question, "What would you do if you had a million dollars?"

Each show began with Tipton sitting in an elegant, high-backed chair in his study at his 60,000-acre estate, Silverstone, where he would describe the next beneficiary to personal secretary Michael Anthony (Marvin Miller), dispensing a few words of wisdom along the way. With veteran announcer Paul Frees providing the voice, audiences saw only the back of Tipton's head or his arm resting on the chair.

Anthony then tracked down the recipient, occasionally receiving a punch in the mouth or a rude brush-off when announcing his gift. Once he convinced the beneficiary that he wasn't kidding, Anthony informed him or her of the conditions accompanying the check: no attempt to learn the identity of the donor was to be made as he wanted to remain anonymous and the amount of the donation was to be kept from everyone but the recipient's spouse. If these stipulations were not honored, the money was forfeit.

The 30-minute show started in January 1955 and ran for five years on Wednesday nights. Miller regularly received mail requests from people applying for their own million dollars, which he typically answered with a letter offering "a million dollars' worth of good luck." The show was syndicated for several years under the title, *If You Had a Million*. In 1978, CBS created a two-hour movie, *The Millionaire*, based on the series and starring Robert Quarry as Michael Anthony.

The Millionaire (CBS), 1955–1960. Michael Anthony: Marvin Miller.

Have Gun, Will Travel

Richard Boone as intellectual gun-for-hire Paladin is seen here defending a woman and her son (guest actors Norma Crane and Johnny Eimen) against the notorious gunman who is the head of their household.

Have Gun, Will Travel featured the Western's most intellectual central character, Paladin, a gun-for-hire who was well versed in literature, history, fine food, and opera.

Paladin (Richard Boone) had been educated at West Point, but he ditched his military career after the Civil War and set out for the adventure of the Old West. He chose the swanky Hotel Carlton in San Francisco as his base and made up business cards featuring a paladin (the white knight of a chess game) and the slogan, "Have Gun, Will Travel . . . Wire Paladin, San Francisco." He sported a thin moustache and dapper apparel, except when on assignment; then he dressed menacingly in black. He quoted Shakespeare and Horace, could name the ingredients of a perfume with a single sniff, and seemed to find killing distasteful, though he did it well—quickly and without muss. He had a gentleman's ethics.

The show's only other recurring role belonged to Kam Tong, who played a hotel employee named Hey Boy. Most episodes started with Hey Boy delivering a handwritten message to Paladin from a prospective client. Tong left in 1960/61 to star in another series, *Mr. Garlund*, but returned the following season. His one year replacement was Lisa Lu, who played—what else?—Hey Girl.

The 30-minute CBS series premiered in 1957 on Saturday nights and was an immediate hit. From 1958–1961, it was the number three program on TV, ranking just behind *Gunsmoke* and *Wagon Train*. Even its theme song, "The Ballad of Paladin," was a hit for performer Johnny Western. The show left the air in September 1963.

In the 1970s, a former rodeo cowboy and Rhode Island radio announcer named Victor De Costa claimed Paladin was based on a character he created in the 1940s and successfully sued CBS for a portion of the program's profits.

Have Gun, Will Travel (CBS), 1957–1963. Paladin: Richard Boone, Hey Boy: Kam Tong (1957–1960; 1961–1963), Hey Girl: Lisa Lu (1960/61).

Perry Mason

Fred MacMurray and Efrem Zimbalist, Jr. were among those considered for the role of defense attorney Perry Mason, but it went to former movie bad guy Raymond Burr, seen here cross-examining a witness.

Perry Mason is fiction's best-known trial lawyer. Created by novelist Erle Stanley Gardner in 1933, Mason began as the central character in a series of novels and in the 1940s evolved into the basis for several feature films and a long-running radio serial. The radio show was part soap opera, part courtroom drama, which the producers split into two CBS television shows: the daytime soap, *The Edge of Night*, which started in 1956 and the prime-time drama, *Perry Mason*, which premiered in 1957.

Fred MacMurray and Efrem Zimbalist, Jr. were among those considered for the lead, but it went to former movie bad guy Raymond Burr, who initially tested for the part of District Attorney Hamilton Burger.

With the help of devoted secretary Della Street (Barbara Hale) and investigator Paul Drake (William Hopper, son of Hollywood columnist Hedda Hopper),

A publicity photo of William Talman as prosecuting attorney Hamilton Burger highlights the one time during the series' 10-year run when Perry Mason lost a case. Of course, Mason eventually coaxed a confession from the guilty party and set his client free.

The defense team celebrates another victory. Pictured with Burr are William Hopper (left) as investigator Paul Drake and Barbara Hale (second from left) as Mason's devoted secretary, Della Street.

Mason typically managed to prove that his clients didn't commit the murder by drawing a courtroom confession from the true culprit. The show usually ended with Mason explaining to Street and Drake how he pieced together the puzzle from a few sketchy clues. Of the 271 cases tried during the series' ten-year run, the defense attorney lost only one, in 1963, and then only because his client wouldn't divulge the evidence which would prove her innocent. Mason eventually coaxed a confession from the guilty party and set her free. Over the years, series guest stars included Robert Redford in 1960 and Ryan O'Neal in 1964.

Perry Mason became a Top 20 show its second season and remained there through the 1961/62 season, when it peaked at number five. A move to Thursday nights in 1962 hurt the ratings. The show fared even worse in 1965 after CBS pitted it against the top-rated *Bonanza* and it was canceled at the end of the season. In 1973, CBS brought back *The New Perry Mason*, starring Monte Markham in the title role (Burr was on rival NBC in *Ironsides*). It lasted one season. In 1985, Burr revived the role in a successful made-for-TV movie for CBS, and several more TV movies have followed.

Perry Mason (CBS), 1957–1966. Perry Mason: Raymond Burr, Della Street: Barbara Hale, Paul Drake: William Hopper, Hamilton Burger: William Talman, Lt. Arthur Tragg: Ray Collins (1957–1965), David Gideon: Karl Held (1960–1962), Lt. Anderson: Wesley Lau (1961–1965), Lt. Steve Drumm: Richard Anderson (1965–1966), Sgt. Brice: Lee Miller (1965–1966), Terrence Clay: Dan Tobin (1965–1966).

For a period piece based on Alexander Woolcott's *The Vanishing Lady*, Hitchcock cast his own daughter, Pat, seen here in a tense moment.

The opening of each episode of *Alfred Hitchcock Presents* found the Master of Suspense in some peculiar situation or another. Here he is enjoying the 1957 Christmas present given to him by the sponsor he never stopped needling.

Alfred Hitchcock Presents

Alfred Hitchcock had been a popular and critically revered film director (*Psycho*, *Rear Window*, *The Birds*) for three decades when CBS brought his black humor and macabre touch to television in 1955. His stories unfolded with suspenseful plot twists and ended in terror. Evil usually prevailed, and Hitchcock got around strict network moral codes by adding an epilogue in which he explained how the villain got his or her just reward eventually.

Alfred Hitchcock Presents (CBS), 1955–1960, 1962–1964; (NBC), 1960–1962, 1964–1965. Host: Alfred Hitchcock.

Before he found movie stardom, Charles Bronson guest-starred on a 1956 episode of Alfred Hitchcock Presents. Estelle Winwood appeared with him as an old woman whose fortune he coveted.

Hitchcock introduced each segment in his trademark clipped British accent. First, the camera would show his silhouette as he filled a line drawing of his round body. Then he'd hint at the plot with pithy, sardonic wordplay before shooting a veiled barb at the show's sponsor.

In truth, Hitchcock directed only 20 of the more than one hundred original episodes shown between 1955 and 1965. Other directors included Robert Altman (*M*A*S*H*, *Nashville*), who worked on several of the programs during the late 1950s. Many future box-office stars appeared in episodes, including Steve McQueen, Robert Redford, Judy Canova, Dick Van Dyke, Cloris Leachman, Peter Fonda, Gena Rowlands, and Brian Keith.

The show enjoyed its greatest success in the late 1950s. In 1960, it moved to NBC for two years. Then CBS bought it back, expanding the former 30-minute program into *The Alfred Hitchcock Hour*. It returned to NBC as an hour-long series in 1964, then was canceled at the end of the season.

Efrem Zimbalist, Jr. and Roger Smith (front seat l. and r.) first played suave, swinging detectives in the show named for the address of their office. The carhop at the restaurant next-door was played by Edd Byrnes (back seat), who later became a detective too.

Efrem Zimbalist, Jr. first played suave detective Stu Bailey in a 1957 episode of *Conflict*, an anthology series on ABC. In 1958, the network gave him a partner, Jeff Spencer (Roger Smith), and put him to work in an office located at 77 Sunset Strip in Hollywood.

Bailey was a refined, Ivy League Ph.D. and a former intelligence officer fluent in several languages. Spencer also came from the Secret Service and had a law degree.

A secondary character, Gerald Lloyd ("Kookie") Kookson III (Edd Byrnes), quickly became an audience favorite and took an increasingly central role. Kookie, a jive-talking carhop at a swanky restaurant next-door to 77 Sunset Strip, was a villain in the first episode. As time passed, he grew into a likable, comic character who regularly assisted Bailey and Spencer while longing to be a detective. He also introduced his own language of "Kookie-isms," most of it adapted from teen slang: "the ginchiest" meant the greatest, "play like a pigeon" meant delivering a message, and "keep the eyeballs rolling" meant being on the lookout. "Kookie, Kookie, Lend Me Your Comb," a song he performed as part of a 1959 episode, became a pop hit for Byrnes and duet partner Connie Stevens.

When Byrnes walked off the set in 1960, demanding a larger role, he was briefly replaced by Troy Donahue, but audience reaction led to his return within a few months. He became a third partner in the detective firm in 1961.

By its second season, *77 Sunset Strip* was ranked among the top 10 programs. More importantly, it grabbed a fanatic following among teenagers and young adults. Having discovered a lucrative market, Warner Brothers immediately developed other programs with hip detectives working in sunny locales. The new series included *Hawaiian Eye*, with Kookie's duet partner, Connie Stevens, in the cast; *Surfside Six*, with Kookie-reject Troy Donahue in a starring role; and *Bourbon Street Beat*. Other studios followed suit, with the likes of *Peter Gunn*, *Checkmate*, and, a bit later on, *Burke's Law*.

The glut of shows apparently wore out the audience. *77 Sunset Strip* slipped from the Top 20 in 1961. In 1963, Jack Webb stepped in as producer and revamped the show, with Zimbalist the lone-remaining cast member. The show was canceled at the end of that season. Reruns of the early shows ran on ABC in the summer of 1964.

77 Sunset Strip (ABC), 1958–1964. Stuart Bailey: Efrem Zimbalist, Jr., Jeff Spencer: Roger Smith (1958–1963), Gerald Lloyd ("Kookie") Kookson III: Edd Byrnes (1958–1963), Roscoe: Louis Guinn (1958–1963), Suzanne Fabray: Jacqueline Beer (1958–1963), Lt. Gilmore: Byron Keith (1958–1963), Rex Randolph: Richard Long (1960–1961), J.R. Hale: Robert Logan (1961–1963), Hannah: Joan Staley (1963–1964).

Variety Shows

The Jack Benny Program

Thereafter, Benny hosted an occasional special until his death in 1974.

The Jack Benny Program (CBS), 1950–1964; (NBC) 1964/1965.

Meyer Kubelsky had already changed his name to Jack Benny when he began appearing on network radio programs in 1932. By 1950, when CBS tentatively began featuring his show on television as well, he was one of America's favorite humorists. But, unlike the talents of several other radio stars, Benny's distinctive timing and memorable mannerisms worked even better on the tube.

His trademarks included an exasperated expression accompanied by propping a hand to his cheek, a pregnant pause, and the exclamation, "Well!" Other famous traits included his character's inept violin playing, his stinginess, his vanity (especially about his age), and references to his prized Maxwell automobile.

The TV format was set up as a situation comedy, but it periodically allowed celebrity guests to sing and dance. Humphrey Bogart, Marilyn Monroe, and Johnny Carson are among those who made their network TV debuts on the series.

Although Benny's show aired regularly from 1950 on, it wasn't broadcast weekly until 1960. NBC immediately picked it up after CBS canceled it in 1964, but it was dropped after one season.

Perhaps no two 1950s comedians offered a greater contrast in styles than Jack Benny (left) and Bob Hope. Where the latter was fast-talking and topical, the former had a slow rhythm and a slate of sure-fire subject areas and gags. But both men were extremely popular on TV.

(Page 93) Sid Caesar and Imogene Coca of Your Show of Shows.

Bing Crosby (left) and George Burns (right) joined Benny for a vaudeville number on a March 1954 episode of the celebrated miser's long-running series.

The original host of *The Tonight Show* was Steve Allen, who presided over the proceedings from 1954 to 1957.

The Tonight Show

In 1953, executives at WNBT-TV in New York had an idea. Why not build upon Steve Allen's multiple talents by asking the musician-writer-comedian to host a late-night program blending comic monologues, musical interludes, and interviews with celebrities?

The 90-minute show came on the air at 11:30 p.m. Monday through Friday, and the concept has outlasted Allen and several subsequent hosts to become the longest-running nighttime series in television history.

Originally known as *The Steve Allen Show*, the live program found Allen behind a desk, where he joked about topical subjects, talked to announcer Gene Rayburn and orchestra leader Skitch Henderson, and brought out a few guests, focusing on musicians, movie stars, and comedians. After 15 months on WNBT, NBC brought the show to a national audience and changed the name to *Tonight!*

Given a weekly prime-time variety show on NBC in 1956, Allen reduced his *Tonight!* appearances to three times a week and then quit altogether in January 1957. For seven months NBC replaced the show with *Tonight: America After Dark*, which was modeled on the news format of the network's morning show, *Today*, and hosted by *Today* alumnus Jack Lescoulie. The new *Tonight* was not successful with viewers or critics.

Deciding to return to the previous format in 1957 NBC began interviewing potential new hosts, eventually choosing CBS game show personality Jack Paar. *The Jack Paar Tonight Show* premiered in July 1957 with a star who was as much an interviewer as a comic. Paar often engaged his guests in serious discussions, in time drawing a reputation for his emotional manner and occasional explosive outbursts. People tuned in because they never knew what Jack would do. He might cry during a poignant interview, then the next night berate a guest for his or her views.

Paar left the show in tearful protest for a month in 1960, then quit for good amid several controversies in 1962. The name was changed to *The Tonight Show* and five months later Johnny Carson took over as host.

The Tonight Show (NBC), 1954– . Hosts: Steve Allen (1954–1957), Ernie Kovacs (1956–1957), Jack Lescoulie (1957), Al "Jazzbo" Collins (1957), Jack Paar (1957–1962), Johnny Carson (1962–1992).

Jack Paar, who took over as the *Tonight Show* host in 1957, was a unique character. He could laugh uproariously, as he is doing here with a favorite guest, Alexander King, or turn maudlin. One simply never knew what he was going to do—which is why millions of viewers tuned in every night.

In the beloved *Honeymooners* portion of the *Gleason* show, Brooklyn's favorite bus driver, Ralph Kramden (Gleason), enjoyed a stormy but loving relationship with his wife, Alice (Audrey Meadows), and his friend, Ed Norton (Art Carney). Norton's wife, Trixie (Joyce Randolph), is at right.

The Jackie Gleason Show

Jackie Gleason had swaggered colorfully through vaudeville, Broadway, and films when he took the lead role in the short-lived, original version of *Life of Riley* in 1949. By the next year, he was a regular on the variety show *Cavalcade of Stars*, one of the few money-makers on the under-financed Dumont network. In 1952, CBS offered Gleason a $6,000-a-week raise to host his own variety show, and he took it.

Other *Cavalcade* colleagues came with the outsized comic to *The Jackie Gleason Show*, including sidekick Art Carney, the June Taylor Dancers, and the Ray Bloch Orchestra. Gleason used the opportunity to expand the characters he created for Dumont. These creations, which to one degree or another reflected Gleason's ability to capture the humor and pathos of the human condition, included the Poor Soul, Joe the Bartender, the Loudmouth, Reggie Van Gleason III, Rudy the Repairman, and Fenwick Babbitt.

But it was another character that Gleason originally debuted on *Cavalcade* that would become his most illustrious. *The Honeymooners* first appeared as a skit in 1951 featuring Gleason as bus driver Ralph Kramden, Carney as upstairs neighbor and sewer worker Ed Norton, and Pert Kelton as Ralph's wife, Alice. Gleason revived *The Honeymooners* as a segment of his CBS series the first season, hiring Audrey Meadows as Alice and Joyce Randolph as Norton's wife, Trixie.

After three years, Gleason wanted a break from the rigors of a weekly, hour-long program. *The Honeymooners* and *Stage Show* (also a Gleason production) replaced his variety series in 1955. Ratings were disappointing, however, and *The Jackie Gleason Show* was revived for a year before another hiatus in 1957. The show returned again 12 months later in an abbreviated, 30-minute slot; this version ended after three months.

Gleason hosted a disastrous quiz show (*You're in the Picture*) in 1961 that he canceled after one week. It was replaced by an interview program, entitled *The Jackie Gleason Show*, that lasted three months. The following fall, the star restored his credibility with a successful variety series, *The Jackie Gleason Show: American Scene Magazine*. The Glea-Girls, the June Taylor Dancers, and the orchestra returned, as did many of Gleason's old characters.

Gleason moved production to Miami in 1964 so that he could play golf year-round. In 1966, Carney returned to to the cast, and the old partners rekindled *The Honeymooners* with Sheila McRae as Alice and Jane Kean as Trixie. For the last four seasons, *The Honeymooners* accounted for more than half of the hour-long telecasts. Some of the episodes were treated as mini-musicals while others retained the straight sitcom format of the originals. Some episodes also took place outside of Brooklyn, unleashing the Kramdens and Nortons on outposts around the world.

The Jackie Gleason Show (CBS), 1952–1958; 1962–1970. Cast: Jackie Gleason, Art Carney (1952–1957, 1966–1970), Joyce Randolph (1952–1957), Audrey Meadows (1952–1957), Buddy Hackett (1958–1959), Frank Fontaine (1962–1966), Sue Ane Langdon (1962–1963), Barbara Heller (1963–1965), Horace McMahon (1963–1964), Alice Ghostley (1962–1964), George Jessel (1965–1966), Sheila MacRae (1966–1970), Jane Kean (1966–1970).

On Cavalcade of Stars and later his own series, Gleason developed a number of characters, which to one degree or another reflected his ability to capture the humor and pathos of the human condition. Among them was Reggie Van Gleason III.

He was awkward and had a peculiar way of speaking, but columnist Ed Sullivan became the host of one of the longest-running shows in television history.

The Ed Sullivan Show

Ed Sullivan was an unlikely variety show host. He couldn't sing, dance, or tell jokes. His diction was peculiar, he had a granite-like face, and he was physically awkward in front of a camera. However, he had been a syndicated columnist for the *New York Daily News*, and like several entertainment journalists, he had been invited to host a radio program in the 1940s. When CBS moved into live television in 1948, they brought Sullivan and his *Toast of the Town* to the tube.

The Moiseyev Dancers were one of a host of exotic acts to appear on The Ed Sullivan Show. The weekly variety program indeed offered viewers an eclectic bill of fare.

Sullivan's first Sunday night show had a budget of $475. The music-and-comedy team of Dean Martin and Jerry Lewis were paid $200; the Broadway musical team, Richard Rodgers and Oscar Hammerstein II, performed for free. The June Taylor Dancers appeared as "The Toastettes," and Sullivan interviewed a fight referee. The budget grew, of course, and in 1955 CBS changed the name to *The Ed Sullivan Show*. But the format stayed the same. Sullivan presented ballet and opera along with dancing bears and a mechanical mouse who told jokes. He followed rock bands with dramatic scenes from Broadway plays. Along the way, he became an American institution, hosting his Sunday night show for 23 years.

The list of celebrities who made their first TV appearances on the program includes Bob Hope, Jack Benny, Humphrey Bogart, Jackie Gleason, Charles Laughton, Maria Callas, Lena Horne, Dinah Shore, Rudolph Nureyev, Margot Fonteyn, the Bolshoi Ballet,

and the Beatles. Although Elvis Presley had been on TV several times earlier, his performance on the Sullivan show is among TV's most famous moments. Sullivan's show ranked among the top 20 programs for 13 seasons between 1953 to 1967. Its highest ratings came in the mid-1950s. Though the program fell from the top 20 in 1968, it continued to draw a large audience. CBS canceled it in 1971 as part of a move toward newer shows designed to attract younger audiences. Sullivan hosted several specials before dying of cancer in 1974 at age 72.

The Ed Sullivan Show (CBS), 1948–1971. Host: Ed Sullivan.

Your Show of Shows became well known for its takeoffs of movies and plays, including *From Here to Eternity*, *A Streetcar Named Desire*, and *High Noon*. Here Sid Caesar and Imogene Coca spoof what appears to be *White Cargo*, the Walter Pigeon–Hedy Lamar film.

Your Show of Shows

Producer Max Liebman first hired comic actors Sid Caesar and Imogene Coca in the mid-1940s for vaudeville revues that he staged in the Catskill Mountains and in Florida. In 1949, when Liebman created *The Admiral Broadway Revue* for television, he teamed the two actors as co-stars.

The Admiral Broadway Revue started in January 1949 and ran simultaneously on NBC and the Dumont network. The series depended strongly on comic monologues and satires with dance, opera, or some other form of highbrow entertainment featured between laughs.

In 1950, NBC gained exclusive rights to the show and persuaded Liebman to expand to 90 minutes and change the name to *Your Show of Shows*. Initially, the program followed *The Jack Carter Show* and was promoted by NBC under an overall title, *Saturday Night Revue*. Carter's show was canceled after the first season. *Your Show of Shows*, however, went on to gain a reputation as one of TV's brightest, most freewheeling comedy series.

Your Show of Shows was the first variety program with a full theater audience, the first with a regular stock company, the first with exclusive scenery and props. While each show featured a special guest, the majority of the program focused on Caesar, Coca, Howard Morris, and Carl Reiner in satirical skits.

A master of dialects and pantomime, Caesar created dozens of recurring characters, including Professor Sigmund von Fraidy Katz, Italian filmmaker Giuseppe Marinara, writer Somerset Winterset, and jazz musician Progress Hornsby. The Caesar-Coca duo portrayed a mismatched married couple, the Hickenloopers. Most shows also featured a satire on a movie or play, including takeoffs on *From Here to Eternity*, *Shane*, *A Streetcar Named Desire*, *A Place in the Sun*, and *High Noon*.

Years later, the show also became famous for its writing staff. Neil Simon, Woody Allen, Larry Gelbart, and Mel Brooks were among those who joined the four stars in coming up with skits. "It was a mad environment in the best sense of the word," said Gelbart, who went on to work on *The Mary Tyler Moore Show* and the films *Tootsie*, *Terms of Endearment*, *Broadcast News*, and the Broadway musical, *A Funny Thing Happened on the Way to the Forum*. "We often compared it to jazz, because it really had that kind of improvisational back-and-forth rhythm."

In 1954, when the show ended after 160 live telecasts, Caesar and Coca started individual shows:

Caesar's Hour lasted three seasons, and the 30-minute *Imogene Coca Show* ended after one season. The four original co-stars reunited in 1958 on *Sid Caesar Invites You*, but the audience and the magic didn't return.

Your Show of Shows (NBC), 1950–1954. Cast: Sid Caesar, Imogene Coca, Carl Reiner, Howard Morris (1951–1954), Robert Merrill (1950–1951), Marguerite Piazza (1950–1953), Bill Hayes (1950–1953), Jerry Ross and Nellie Fisher (1950–1952), Mata and Hari (1950–1953).

One of Caesar's recurring characters was a nutty German professor called Sigmund von Fraidy Katz, who was usually interviewed by the show's second banana, Carl Reiner.

The host of *American Bandstand* throughout its 30-year network run was the ever-young Dick Clark. He is pictured here in the show's early days with Ruth Brown.

American Bandstand

Originally called *Bandstand*, it began as a regional show on Philadelphia's WFIL-TV with host Bob Horn. The set looked like a record shop, and local teens danced to current pop hits between film clips of national performers. Dick Clark, a popular Philly disc jockey, took over in 1956.

In the summer of 1957, ABC began offering it as a daily afternoon program to its affiliates. That fall, the network premiered a Monday night version. Although the prime-time *American Bandstand* failed, an identical show aired on Monday–Friday afternoons and it proved as popular with teens as the rock 'n' roll music it featured.

Dick Clark didn't start *American Bandstand*, but his shrewd business sense and uncanny knowledge of the youth market helped develop it into a TV staple for three decades.

Much of the action of American Bandstand centered around the dance floor, where teens showed off the latest steps.

The formula featured Clark introducing a couple of guest performers who would lip-sync one or two of their hits, gab about their careers, and sign autographs. An up-and-coming pop song was introduced and rated by two members of the audience, creating the famous response: "It's got a good beat, and you can dance to it." The rest of the show featured young cast members dancing to current songs.

American Bandstand held to its daily after-school schedule until 1963, when ABC shifted it to Saturdays, where it remained until 1987. That year, ABC wanted to cut the hour-long show to 30 minutes, but Clark decided to maintain the full hour and offer new programs in syndication. After 18 struggling months, the USA Network picked up it up and aired it on cable on Saturday afternoons. At that point, Clark retired from hosting, giving the microphone to 26-year-old David Hirsch, who was the same age as Clark had been when he joined the program. USA canceled after 26 weeks.

American Bandstand (ABC), 1957–1987. Host: Dick Clark.

The Red Skelton Show

San Fernando Red (Skelton, center) presides over the courtroom where gueststar Raymond Burr (of Perry Mason fame) attempts to represent his client, Fifi (Julie Redding). The judge seems more interested in the defendant than the lawyer, however.

As a radio star in the 1940s, Red Skelton was famous for the variety of exaggerated voices he gave to the comical characters he created. In the 1950s, he proved his characters could be even more colorful when he was allowed to add broad physical gestures. As host of *The Red Skelton Show*, the comedian distorted his face, tripped around the stage, and endeared himself to America.

One of Skelton's many recurring characters was bumbling George Appleby, seen here putting the finishing touches on his robot, Josephine. The episode aired in June 1957.

When NBC offered Skelton his first series in 1951, the red-headed son of a circus clown brought with him most of the personalities he created during the previous 10 years on radio. They included the flustered old-timer Clem Kadiddlehopper, the Mean Whiddle Kid, the con man San Fernando Red, the off-target Sheriff Deadeye, the punch-drunk boxer Cauliflower McPugg, and the bumbling drunk Willie Lump-Lump. He also came up with new characters, including Freddie the Freeloader, the tender hobo whom Skelton portrayed through pantomime. The show's only other regular was orchestra leader David Rose, whom Skelton kept with him from his radio days and on through 20 years of TV.

In its first year on NBC in 1951, *The Red Skelton Show* ranked as TV's fourth most popular program, winning an Emmy Award for best comedy scenes and another for its host as best comedian. In 1953, CBS lured Skelton to its network and put his 30-minute show on Tuesday nights without changing the title or format. In 1962, the show expanded to 60 minutes and, two years later, the name was changed to *The Red Skelton Hour*.

From 1955 to 1970, the show annually ranked among TV's 20 top-rated series, with its peak popularity coming in the mid-1960s. It remained a most popular series when canceled in 1970 by CBS as the network switched to more youth-oriented programming. Skelton returned to NBC in 1971 to host a 30-minute variety show featuring a large cast. It was canceled after one season.

The Red Skelton Show (NBC), 1951–1953; (CBS), 1953–1970; (NBC), 1970–1971. Host: Red Skelton.

Of the many characters at Skelton's command, perhaps the best loved was Freddie the Freeloader, the tender hobo portrayed through pantomime.

The intimacy of television was perfect for Perry Como, whose relaxed manner, casual attire, and easy way with a song made his show a popular favorite for 15 years.

The customers who stopped by Pierino Como's barbershop in the small mining town of Canonsburg, Pennsylvania in the late 1920s used to request a song along with their shaves and trims. The ambitious shop owner had started cutting hair at age 14, and by the time he turned 21 in 1933, he closed his business for a few days to travel to Cleveland to audition as a vocalist in the Freddy Carlone band. After getting the job, he began performing under his nickname, Perry.

Within three years, Como was with the Ted Weems orchestra, one of the most popular groups of the big band era. When World War II forced the band to split up in 1942, the singer returned to his Canonsburg barbershop. Before long, however, he received a call from a talent agent who wanted him to host a show on NBC radio and, as part of the deal, sign with the parent company's record label, RCA Victor. By the time TV came along, Como's smooth, relaxed style had made him one of America's biggest stars.

In 1948, he began hosting *The Chesterfield Supper Club*, a 15-minute live NBC program that, initially, simply stuck a camera in the radio studio and telecast Como and guests at the microphone with scripts in hand. CBS lured the singer to host a three-times-a-week show in 1950, and it lasted until NBC brought him back five years later and set him up with his own weekly, hour-long series.

The Perry Como Show always opened with the singer crooning the theme, "Dream Along with Me (I'm on My Way to a Star)," and usually featured a request segment introduced by a group of anonymous women singing, "Letters, we get letters, stacks and stacks of letters." The ending often featured Como doing a religious or serious ballad that led into his traditional closer, "You Are Never Far Away from Me."

The NBC series enjoyed its greatest success from 1955-1958, and it proved more enduring than similar programs hosted by other popular singers (Dinah Shore, Rosemary Clooney, Kate Smith, and Andy Williams). In 1961, Kraft took over as sponsor and added several young comics to the cast, including Kaye Ballard, Don Adams, Paul Lynde, Sandy Stewart, and Jack Duffy. Announcer Frank Gallop, with the show through its eight-year run, also played a prominent role as Como's comic foil. After NBC canceled the series in 1963, Como went on to host several *Kraft Music Hall* specials.

The Perry Como Show (NBC), 1948–1950; (CBS), 1950–1955; (NBC), 1955–1963. Cast: Perry Como, Fontane Sisters (1948–1954), Ray Charles Singers (1950–1963), Kaye Ballard (1961–1963), Don Adams (1961–1963), Sandy Stewart (1961–1963), Jack Duffy (1961–1963), Paul Lynde (1961–1962), Pierre Olaf (1962–1963).

The Garry Moore Show

Garry Moore was one of radio's most popular hosts in the early days of American broadcasting. He took his first important radio job in the medium in 1939, and through the 1940s starred in several radio shows, including *Club Matinee*, *Take It or Leave It*, and *The Jimmy Durante-Garry Moore Show*. On *Club Matinee* he made two important career moves: he suggested a contest to replace his real name, Thomas Garrison Morfit, with a catchier moniker; and he teamed up with his longtime sidekick, comedian Durward Kirby.

In June 1950, CBS began simulcasting *The Garry Moore Show* on television and radio five days a week. In the fall of 1951, the weeknight show was moved to an afternoon time slot; at the same time, *The Garry Moore Evening Show* began on Wednesday nights featuring the same variety format and cast of singers, dancers, and comics. By 1952, the evening show had ended, but the enduring daytime program continued until June 1958.

The daytime show provided early television exposure for many performers who went on to greater fame, including Don Adams, Kaye Ballard, Wally Cox, George Gobel, Don Knotts, Peter Marshall, Leslie Uggams, a 12-year-old Tuesday Weld, and Jonathan Winters. He also introduced Carol Burnett by giving her a regular role starting in 1956.

By 1958, Moore had tired of the daily grind—he also had been hosting a prime-time quiz show, *I've Got a Secret*, for six years. After a summer vacation, he returned in a prime-time CBS variety program, *The Garry Moore Show*. The veteran still sported his trademark crew cut and bow tie, and he still displayed the same informal, relaxed manner of his previous program. He also brought back Kirby, Burnett, and comic Marion Lorne as regular cast members. After six successful seasons, Moore again grew weary; he ended the variety show and left the quiz show. An attempt to revive the variety program in 1966 failed to reclaim his audience, but Moore went on to host the popular daytime game show, *To Tell the Truth*.

The Garry Moore Show (CBS), 1950–1958; 1958–1964; 1966–1967.

Garry Moore was not a singer, dancer, comedian, actor, or—this photo notwithstanding—musician. But he could do a bit of everything, had a relaxed, friendly manner, and surrounded himself with a group of highly talented regulars including, in 1956, a very young Carol Burnett.

Texaco Star Theater

Uncle Miltie does a soft-shoe with swimming star Esther Williams in a 1955 episode of what was then called *The Milton Berle Show*. At the outset of that season Berle and company had moved to Hollywood, where the show had become the first color series telecast nationally from the West Coast.

Milton Berle—nicknamed "Mr. Television"—was the first major network star. A show business veteran, he had appeared in vaudeville, films, and as the host of the *Texaco Star Theater* on the NBC radio network. But it was the tube that made him a household name.

Audiences reacted strongly to this rubber-faced, slapstick comic who dressed in outrageous costumes and willingly subjected himself to an endless series of embarrassing situations. So taken were people with Uncle Miltie's weekly antics, that Berle, all by himself, created a sales boom for TV sets: total sales topped the million mark for the first time a few months after he took over as weekly host of the *Texaco* show.

On Tuesday nights, when Berle's show aired, a hush fell over public nightspots. Streets emptied. People crowded into living rooms graced with the large consoles of the day. Some neighbors even put their tubes into front windows so the whole block could enjoy the show.

Initially, Berle shared the hosting chores on the *Texaco Star Theater*, rotating with comics Henny Youngman, Jack Carter, Morey Amsterdam, Georgie Price, and Harry Richman. After three months, Berle had become the clear favorite and took over as weekly star in the fall of 1948.

Texaco Star Theater remained TV's highest-rated program until 1951. That year, Berle signed a contract with NBC guaranteeing him $200,000 annually for the next 30 years. Reflecting its star's stature, *The Texaco Star Theater* became *The Milton Berle Show* in 1953. Two years later it moved to Hollywood and became the first series telecast nationally in color from the West Coast. The show ran its course in the spring of 1956, with Elvis Presley making guest appearances in two of the final episodes.

Texaco Star Theater (*The Milton Berle Show*) (NBC), 1948–1956.

Dressing in drag was one of Berle's specialties. Here he is seen as Cleopatra with gueststar Jack Benny as Ben-Hur— an impossible relationship (the fictional Judean prince lived at the time of Christ, long after the Egyptian queen's death).

Acknowledgements

The producers of this book gratefully acknowledge the efforts of the National Broadcasting Company, the Columbia Broadcasting System, the American Broadcasting Company, and the independent production companies, artists, writers, directors, technicians, musicians, and designers whose contribution to the television arts and sciences are celebrated in this book. Thanks, too, are due to Howard Mandelbaum and Ron Mandelbaum of Photofest, and to Harold Clarke of BDD Promotional Book Company, whose idea this was.

By the start of the 1950s, one million television sets were in use in America. Here, in an advertising photo for RCA, a typical family of four enjoys Kukla, Fran and Ollie.